Cinder – Begin Creative Coding

A quick introduction into the world of creative coding with Cinder through basic tutorials and a couple of advanced examples

Krisjanis Rijnieks

BIRMINGHAM - MUMBAI

Cinder – Begin Creative Coding

Copyright © 2013 Packt Publishing

All rights reserved. No part of this book may be reproduced, stored in a retrieval system, or transmitted in any form or by any means, without the prior written permission of the publisher, except in the case of brief quotations embedded in critical articles or reviews.

Every effort has been made in the preparation of this book to ensure the accuracy of the information presented. However, the information contained in this book is sold without warranty, either express or implied. Neither the author, nor Packt Publishing, and its dealers and distributors will be held liable for any damages caused or alleged to be caused directly or indirectly by this book.

Packt Publishing has endeavored to provide trademark information about all of the companies and products mentioned in this book by the appropriate use of capitals. However, Packt Publishing cannot guarantee the accuracy of this information.

First published: February 2013

Production Reference: 1150213

Published by Packt Publishing Ltd.
Livery Place
35 Livery Street
Birmingham B3 2PB, UK.

ISBN 978-1-84951-956-4

www.packtpub.com

Cover Image by J.Blaminsky (milak6@wp.pl)

Credits

Author
Krisjanis Rijnieks

Reviewers
Reinis Adovičs
Nikolas

Acquisition Editor
Joanne Fitzpatrick

Commissioning Editor
Yogesh Dalvi

Technical Editors
Sharvari Baet
Prasad Dalvi

Project Coordinator
Joel Goveya

Proofreader
Amy Guest

Indexer
Tejal R. Soni

Production Coordinator
Conidon Miranda
Shantanu Zagade

Cover Work
Conidon Miranda

About the Author

Krisjanis Rijnieks is a new media professional with a background in painting and multimedia. He holds a BA in painting, and parallel to his painting studies he has been doing a lot of things related to print, video, web, flash, Flash coding, and coding in general. It is not possible to name all the different categories of work but through all this a strong interest towards interactive digital media has been developed.

Creative coding is a new field that brings the art and design fields much closer to the one which is called coding. As he has been doing things on both sides, the combination of the two seemed natural. It is a way of using ones creative visual and logical skills together without worrying that an unsolvable conflict between the left and right side of the brain will occur.

For the past two years, he has been involved in many projects that include creative coding with technologies such as Flash ActionScript, openFrameworks, Cinder, iOS, Unity 3D, Kinect, Augmented Reality, Quartz Composer, VDMX, and projection mapping with MadMapper. Experience gathered through these projects required him to search for new and more powerful tools and skills constantly. Cinder is one of the tools that allows one to combine the hottest topics of todays computer science (computer vision, gesture recognition, and so on) with the craziest ideas and make them work in real time without acceleration lags.

Currently he is studying the New Media MA program at the Aalto University School of Art, Design, and Architecture, also known as the Helsinki Media Lab in Finland. He also does freelancing of commercial projects and is making his first entrepreneurial steps by managing his company called Skematic.

This is the very first book that he has written, and according to him it was fun and rewarding in terms of knowledge and experience.

> First, I would like to thank Packt Publishing and the people behind it for the offer to author this book. To Irina Spicaka for being patient and supportive while writing. Huge respect to Reinis Adovics for being a mad scientist, living the dream of the creative coder through his own company Warp, and for agreeing to be the technical reviewer of this title. Finally I would like to thank Nuno Correia (Lecturer and Researcher of the SOPI Research Group at the Aalto University School of Art, Design and Architecture) for the tips and possibility to combine this with my studies, and the whole Helsinki Media Lab students and crew for showing their interest towards this topic.

About the Reviewers

Reinis Adovičs holds a masters degree in architecture. Although the thesis was on urban planning he also studied algorithmic architecture — parametric, cybernetic design, morphodynamics, biomimetics, digital prototyping, and production. Implementing ideas in the latter was made easier due to the in-depth knowledge and lifelong love for mathematics, exact sciences (he has also got a background in civil engineering), and programming experience.

Therefore the field of creative coding emerged naturally, it is a result of morphing both expressions — humanities and mathematics. But mostly he sees no difference between the two.

Before using code for visualization, he started scripting in the school years in order to organize everyday work more effectively, continued by client-server side utilities in different languages, and more serious apps written in C, C++, and Objective-C. Since then he has touched many coding tools for various purposes.

The first creative coding toolsets he used were Processing (Java) and Quartz Composer. As datasets grew he made the first switch to openFrameworks (C/C++/GLSL). And lately he made the second one — the tool of choice for new projects is Cinder.

He focuses on real-time responsive solutions — physical computing and interactive installations. Currently he is also exploring audio and space reactive VJ-ing.

> I would like to thank the open hardware and software community for the vast knowledge provided that knows no boundaries between the phenomena shaping the world around us. And special thanks to coffee and cigarettes; those things ain't healthy though.

About the Reviewers

Nikolas is a hybrid of a developer, maker, and artist. He holds a BSc in Physics from the University of Kent (UK), an MSc by research in Physics from the same university, and is a recent alumni of the Interactive Telecommunications Program (ITP), Tisch School of the Arts, NYU.

He has worked on interactive projects for Potion (NYC), Pentagram (NYC), FH-Salzburg (AT), Arc Worldwide (GR), and has also taught a Masters level Introduction to Physical Computing course (AT).

His personal projects have been featured at the Come Out and Play Festival 2010 (NYC), the Vimeo Festival and Awards 2010 (NYC), the ITP shows 2009, 2010 (NYC), the 3rd Ward Show 2010 (NYC), the Schmiede Festival 2012 (AT), the Core77 online design gallery, the Engadget and Adafruit websites.

With his work, he is exploring the intersection of art and technology, and aims to push the boundaries between the digital and physical world.

www.PacktPub.com

Support files, eBooks, discount offers and more

You might want to visit www.PacktPub.com for support files and downloads related to your book.

Did you know that Packt offers eBook versions of every book published, with PDF and ePub files available? You can upgrade to the eBook version at www.PacktPub.com and as a print book customer, you are entitled to a discount on the eBook copy. Get in touch with us at service@packtpub.com for more details.

At www.PacktPub.com, you can also read a collection of free technical articles, sign up for a range of free newsletters and receive exclusive discounts and offers on Packt books and eBooks.

http://PacktLib.PacktPub.com

Do you need instant solutions to your IT questions? PacktLib is Packt's online digital book library. Here, you can access, read and search across Packt's entire library of books.

Why Subscribe?

- Fully searchable across every book published by Packt
- Copy and paste, print and bookmark content
- On demand and accessible via web browser

Free Access for Packt account holders

If you have an account with Packt at www.PacktPub.com, you can use this to access PacktLib today and view nine entirely free books. Simply use your login credentials for immediate access.

Table of Contents

Preface	1
Chapter 1: Learn Cinder Basics – Now!	**7**
What is creative coding	7
A few words about Cinder	8
Downloading Cinder	8
Setting up Cinder on Mac OS X	10
Setting up Cinder on Windows	11
Microsoft Visual C++ Express 2010	11
Windows Platform SDK	11
DirectX SDK	12
QuickTime SDK	12
Launching the sample application	13
Summary	14
Chapter 2: Know What is Possible – The Cinder Toolset	**15**
BasicApp	16
BezierPath	17
CairoBasic	21
CaptureTest	23
EaseGallery	24
TextBox	25
ArcballDemo	26
Earthquake	26
AudioGenerative	27
Summary	28
Chapter 3: Initial Setup – Creating the BaseApp	**29**
TinderBox	29

Table of Contents

Creating a project from scratch (Mac OS X)	**31**
Basic project setup (Xcode 3)	32
Basic project setup (Xcode 4+)	33
Adding code (Xcode 3 and 4+)	34
Connecting to Cinder (Xcode 3)	35
Connecting to Cinder (Xcode 4+)	36
Creating a project from scratch (Windows)	**39**
Final adjustments	**41**
Summary	**44**
Chapter 4: Prepare Your Brushes – Drawing Basic Shapes	**45**
Preparing your workspace	45
Drawing lines	47
Drawing circles	49
Drawing rectangles	51
Other useful drawing functions	52
Summary	54
Chapter 5: Making Use of Images – Loading and Displaying	**55**
Loading an image	55
Handling assets	57
Summary	60
Chapter 6: Accelerate – Creating Generative Animation	**61**
Preparing the stage	61
Adding animation	63
Adding randomness	66
More circles	68
Using built-in eases	70
Summary	75
Chapter 7: Working with Images – Real-time Postprocessing and Effects	**77**
Introducing Texture, Surface, and Channel	77
Applying the grayscale effect	78
Using threshold	80
Animating effects	82
Applying effects to moving images	83
Summary	86
Chapter 8: Adding Depth – Cinder 3D Basics	**87**
Introducing the 3D space	87
Drawing in 3D	89

Understanding nested states	**92**
Handling depth sorting	**94**
Exploring other Cinder 3D primitives	**96**
Summary	**99**
Chapter 9: Enter Sound – Adding Sound and Audio	**101**
Loading and playing a sound file	**101**
Using tracks	**102**
Changing track parameters	**103**
Visualizing audio	**105**
Using audio input	**108**
Summary	**109**
Chapter 10: Talk to the User – Adding Interactivity and UI Events	**111**
Handling events	**111**
Using mouseMove()	112
Using mouseDown()	114
Using mouseDrag()	116
Using keyDown()	118
Using fileDrop()	118
Summary	**120**
Appendix: Basic Cinder Functionality Reference	**121**
Basic types	**121**
Applications	**122**
Basic graphics	**124**
Images	**126**
Other functions	**126**
Index	**127**

Preface

Cinder is one of the most powerful open source creative coding frameworks that is available right now on the Internet. It is based on one of the most popular and powerful intermediate-level programming language C++ and relies on minimum third-party libraries. It is a combination of low-level and high-level language features, and that makes it relatively easy to grasp for those who have a higher-level programming language background.

Cinder can be considered the next-level creative coding framework for those who are familiar with Processing, ActionScript, or other similar high-level programming languages or frameworks. Cinder may seem similar to openFrameworks, it is, in terms since it is based on C++, but the philosophy behind the framework is a bit different.

openFrameworks is based on a lot of third-party libraries that do the job and sometimes may make a simple application to be big in size. Cinder is different in terms, that is, it tries to make use of the features of the operating system that it runs on. It does not mean that it is better than openFrameworks, but for some scenarios it may be more efficient than the other one.

Programming is something that rapidly becomes a skill that everyone should know. Estonia just introduced computer programming learning for all children attending school, meaning that everyone from Grades 1 to 12 are learning how to code. It is not hard to believe that there will be a lot of other countries that will follow. This means that in the future computer technology will be everywhere more than it is today and the situation will demand a vast amount of people who will need to take care of it. Another fact is that we most probably will see programming in more and more fields that previously had weak or absolutely no connection to it.

Preface

And that is where creative coding comes in. Creative coding is becoming more and more popular these days as even more people start to appreciate the logical and interactive dimension that programming can give to their work. It is possible to create a painting that paints itself, a live sculpture, or an interactive chair that does not let anyone to sit on it—the possibilities are endless. It is only the matter of ones creativity and programming knowledge.

One thing that is important in todays creative coding frameworks is performance and flexibility. Usually the more powerful and flexible a framework is, the harder it is to learn it. As Cinder is both, flexible, and powerful, it is not an easy task to understand how to use it.

This book is a trial to make the Cinder learning curve less steep. Through a collection of simple guided examples, we will try to cover the basic functionality that is usually provided by other creative coding tools.

What this book covers

Chapter 1, Learn Cinder Basics – Now!, provides a brief introduction about creative coding and Cinder. It will help you to set up and test Cinder on Mac OS X and Windows machines.

Chapter 2, Know What is Possible – The Cinder Toolset, introduces you to various basic tasks that can be performed with Cinder through compiling, running, and discussing some of the Cinder sample applications.

Chapter 3, Initial Setup – Creating the BaseApp, explains how to create a base project by using Cinder's integrated tool TinderBox, and from scratch.

Chapter 4, Prepare Your Brushes – Drawing Basic Shapes, provides insight into Cinder's built-in basic shape drawing functions that are usually there in other creative coding frameworks.

Chapter 5, Making Use of Images – Loading and Displaying, explains loading and displaying of images, which is an important part of every creative coding language. In this chapter we will learn how to load and display images from local and networked storage with Cinder.

Chapter 6, Accelerate – Creating Generative Animation, teaches the basics of generative or procedural animation with Cinder. Throughout the chapter we will create an infinite looped animation application.

Chapter 7, Working with Images – Real-time Postprocessing and Effects, explains the several features that Cinder provides to let you manipulate images, and moving image frames down to the pixel level without loosing speed. In this chapter we will learn how to use Cinder for applying and creating basic effects for still images and real-time use.

Chapter 8, Adding Depth – Cinder 3D Basics, introduces you to the basic 3D aspects and practical methods, as well as the 3D primitives that can be drawn with Cinder.

Chapter 9, Enter Sound – Adding Sound and Audio, explains how to load, modify, play back, and use sound files, as well as live audio input to draw and animate.

Chapter 10, Talk to the User – Adding Interactivity and UI Events, explains how to handle mouse, keyboard, and other events in Cinder.

Appendix A, Basic Cinder Functionality Reference, helps you find some basic Cinder functionality used in this book for later reference.

Bonus Chapter, Escaping Singleness – Communicating with Other Applications, is not present in the book but is available for download at the following link: http://www.packtpub.com/sites/default/files/downloads/Escaping_Singleness.pdf

What you need for this book

All you need is a Mac OS X or Windows computer. The code samples in this book are tested on Mac OS X 10.6+ and Windows 7 machines. There is a list of development software for each operating system and further details about it will be discussed in the following chapters. In this book we will make use of the following software:

Mac OS X

- Xcode 3+ or Xcode 4+
- MadMapper

Windows

- Microsoft Visual C++ 10+
- Windows platform SDK
- DirectX SDK
- QuickTime SDK

Both

- Pure Data

Preface

Who this book is for

This book is for those who want to make a change either from a lower-level creative coding framework or from other kinds of coding to creative coding with Cinder. You will not find an introductory chapter about programming in general in this book, you should know something about it already.

This book is for you if you have previous experience with text-based programming languages such as Processing, ActionScript, JavaScript, or visual ones, such as Pure Data, Max MSP, VVVV, or Quartz Composer.

Conventions

In this book, you will find a number of styles of text that distinguish between different kinds of information. Here are some examples of these styles, and an explanation of their meaning.

Code words in text are shown as follows: "We can include other contexts through the use of the `include` directive."

A block of code is set as follows:

```
void TextBoxApp::render()
{
   string txt = "Here is some text that is larger than can fit
   naturally inside of 100 pixels.\nAnd here is another line after
   a hard break."; [default]
```

When we wish to draw your attention to a particular part of a code block, the relevant lines or items are set in bold:

```
void TextBoxApp::render()
{
   string txt = "Here is some text that is larger than can fit
   naturally inside of 100 pixels.\nAnd here is another line after
   a hard break."; [default]
```

New terms and **important words** are shown in bold. Words that you see on the screen, in menus or dialog boxes for example, appear in the text like this: "clicking the **Next** button moves you to the next screen".

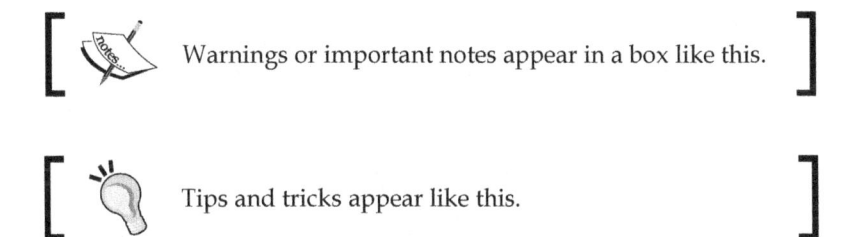

> Warnings or important notes appear in a box like this.

> Tips and tricks appear like this.

Reader feedback

Feedback from our readers is always welcome. Let us know what you think about this book—what you liked or may have disliked. Reader feedback is important for us to develop titles that you really get the most out of.

To send us general feedback, simply send an e-mail to feedback@packtpub.com, and mention the book title via the subject of your message. If there is a topic that you have expertise in and you are interested in either writing or contributing to a book, see our author guide on www.packtpub.com/authors.

Customer support

Now that you are the proud owner of a Packt book, we have a number of things to help you to get the most from your purchase.

Downloading the example code

You can download the example code files for all Packt books you have purchased from your account at http://www.packtpub.com. If you purchased this book elsewhere, you can visit http://www.packtpub.com/support and register to have the files e-mailed directly to you.

Downloading the color images of this book

We also provide you a PDF file that has color images of the screenshots/diagrams used in this book. The color images will help you better understand the changes in the output.

You can download this file from:
http://www.packtpub.com/sites/default/files/downloads/
9564OS_ColoredImages.pdf

Errata

Although we have taken every care to ensure the accuracy of our content, mistakes do happen. If you find a mistake in one of our books—maybe a mistake in the text or the code—we would be grateful if you would report this to us. By doing so, you can save other readers from frustration and help us improve subsequent versions of this book. If you find any errata, please report them by visiting http://www.packtpub.com/submit-errata, selecting your book, clicking on the **errata submission form** link, and entering the details of your errata. Once your errata are verified, your submission will be accepted and the errata will be uploaded on our website, or added to any list of existing errata, under the Errata section of that title. Any existing errata can be viewed by selecting your title from http://www.packtpub.com/support.

Piracy

Piracy of copyright material on the Internet is an ongoing problem across all media. At Packt, we take the protection of our copyright and licenses very seriously. If you come across any illegal copies of our works, in any form, on the Internet, please provide us with the location address or website name immediately so that we can pursue a remedy.

Please contact us at copyright@packtpub.com with a link to the suspected pirated material.

We appreciate your help in protecting our authors, and our ability to bring you valuable content.

Questions

You can contact us at questions@packtpub.com if you are having a problem with any aspect of the book, and we will do our best to address it.

Learn Cinder Basics – Now! 1

In this chapter we will learn:

- What is creative coding
- What is Cinder
- How to set it up on Mac OS X and Windows
- How to test if the setup actually works

What is creative coding

This is a really short introduction about what creative coding is, and I'm sure that it is possible to find out much more about this topic on the Internet. Nevertheless, I will try to explain how it looks from my perspective.

Creative coding is a relatively new term for a field that combines coding and design. The central part of this term might be the "coding" one—to become a creative coder, you need to know how to write code and some other things about programming in general. Another part—the "creative" one—contains design and all the other things that can be combined with coding.

Being skilled in coding and design at the same time lets you explain your ideas as working prototypes for interface designs, art installations, phone applications, and other fields. It can save time and effort that you would give in explaining your ideas to someone else so that he/she could help you. The creative coding approach may not work so well in large projects, unless there are more than one creative codes involved.

A lot of new tools that make programming more accessible have emerged during the last few years. All of them are easy to use, but usually the less complicated a tool is, the less powerful it is, and vice versa.

Cinder is one of the most powerful tools in the world of creative coding. In this chapter, we will learn what Cinder is and how to set it up on the two most popular operating systems—Mac OS X and Windows. If you have access to both and you want to do it as fast as possible, choose Mac OS X. It won't take much longer on Windows, if you have a good Internet connection.

A few words about Cinder

So we are up to some Cinder coding! Cinder is one of the most professional and powerful creative coding frameworks that you can get for free on the Internet. It can help you if you are creating some really complicated interactive real-time audio-visual piece, because it uses one of the most popular and powerful low-level programming languages out there—C++—and relies on minimum third-party code libraries. The creators of Cinder also try to use all the newest C++ language features, even those that are not standardized yet (but soon will be) by using the so called Boost libraries.

This book is not intended as an A-to-Z guide about Cinder nor the C++ programming language, nor areas of mathematics involved. This is a short introduction for us who have been working with similar frameworks or tools and know some programming already. As Cinder relies on C++, the more we know about it the better. Knowledge of ActionScript, Java, or even JavaScript will help you understand what is going on here.

Downloading Cinder

Ok, less talk, do more! Point your browser to the Cinder website (http://libcinder.org).

Chapter 1

Click on the **Download** link in the main menu and choose one of the following two versions depending on your operating system of choice:

- Cinder for Mac OS X (Mac OS X)
- Cinder for Visual C++ 2010 (Windows)

 We will be using the packed Cinder Version 0.8.4 throughout this book, but some differences between it and the newest Cinder Version 0.8.5 will be pointed out.

Now we are going to split the Cinder setup in two groups: Mac OS X and Windows. This is because of the configuration process, which is a bit different for each platform. You will get up and running faster if you use Mac OS X, but it is not blamable in case you appear to use Windows—just get yourself a good Internet connection and you are good to go!

Setting up Cinder on Mac OS X

Setting up Cinder on Mac OS X is relatively easy if you have done some coding before—that means, if you have Xcode installed. If not, you have to download and install it. To do that get yourself an Apple Developer Account from `https://developer.apple.com/programs/register/`.

Once you have your Apple Developer ID and password, go to the Xcode download section at `https://developer.apple.com/xcode/` or open up the App Store application and search for the Xcode application there.

The process of installing Xcode is not a topic that we will be covering in this book, but it should be quite self-explanatory as Apple has a long history of making their applications as user friendly as possible. If you encounter problems with installing Xcode, try Google or go to the official Apple Developer Xcode FAQ located at `https://developer.apple.com/support/xcode/`.

So now you have Xcode installed on your computer! Let's move on and unarchive the downloaded Cinder package at a safe location, for example, `/Users/Your_Username/cinder`. In my case, the path is `/Users/kr15h/cinder`.

Next, we are going to test if our newly created setup is working by opening one of the sample applications. We will try out the QuickTime sample application. To do that open the file `quickTimeSample.xcodeproj` (`QuickTimeBasic.xcodeproj` in Cinder 0.8.5) in the `cinder/samples/QuickTime/xcode/` directory (`cinder/samples/QuickTimeBasic/xcode/` in Cinder 0.8.5). In Xcode, select **Build | Build and Run** (**Product | Run** on Xcode 4+). You can achieve the same effect by pressing *Cmd + R* or by clicking on the **Build and Run** (simply **Run** in Xcode 4+) button in the toolbar (you can recognize it by a round green play button that is placed over a grayscale hammer or a round gray play button in Xcode 4+).

An **Open File** dialog should pop up. Go and select a movie file from your hard drive!

If you see the movie playing back in a window, success! You are ready to move on to the next chapter. If not, try to follow the steps mentioned in this section more carefully — maybe you did not notice something.

Setting up Cinder on Windows

Setting up Cinder on Windows might take a bit longer than on Mac OS X. That does not mean that it will work slower though. The thing that is good about Windows PCs is that you can usually be more elastic with your hardware configuration. So, if you have a strong will to create some wicked generative stuff with the right kind of hardware you choose, go for Windows and equip yourself with some QuadCore CPU, SSD hard drive, and appropriate GPU. It won' t hurt.

The main reason why configuring Cinder in Windows takes more time is that you'll have to download more stuff. Except the Cinder package, you also have to download and install the following.

Microsoft Visual C++ Express 2010

The reason of choosing this IDE is that all the official Cinder sample application projects are created for this one. Here we will use Microsoft Visual C++ as it is the default Windows IDE chosen by Cinder creators.

To download Microsoft Visual C++, point your browser at http://www.microsoft.com/visualstudio/eng/downloads#d-2010-express.

Click on **Visual C++ 2010 Express** tab, choose the language to be downloaded, and click on **Install**. A download should start and when it is finished, open the *.exe file.

We will not cover the whole installation process, as it is not the scope of this book. Just choose the default options for everything and it will be fine. Let's move on to the next component we still need.

Windows Platform SDK

We need this **software development kit** (**SDK**) in order to communicate our programs with the Windows system. The Cinder framework will do it for us, so we won't see anything Windows specific — just multiplatform Cinder specific. Don't be afraid and download the Windows Platform SDK from http://bit.ly/IL35OV.

When the download is complete, do run it! Choose default options everywhere again and everything should be ok.

Learn Cinder Basics – Now!

DirectX SDK

We need this because Cinder audio core relies on it. So let's get it from `http://bit.ly/OSe24s`.

Install with the default settings and you are good to continue.

QuickTime SDK

You do not need to download QuickTime SDK, if you are using Cinder 0.8.5.

You will have to get an Apple Developer Account to download it. Get it from `https://developer.apple.com/programs/register/`.

Then go to `https://developer.apple.com/quicktime/`.

Be careful while installing it. Cinder expects that QuickTime SDK resides in the same directory level (and with the directory name `QuickTimeSDK-7.3`) as Cinder itself. So, if you keep your Cinder in `C:\cinder`, the QuickTime SDK should reside at `C:\QuickTimeSDK-7.3` — change this while installing the SDK.

When you come to a point in the installation where you can choose the destination folder, click on the **Change** button.

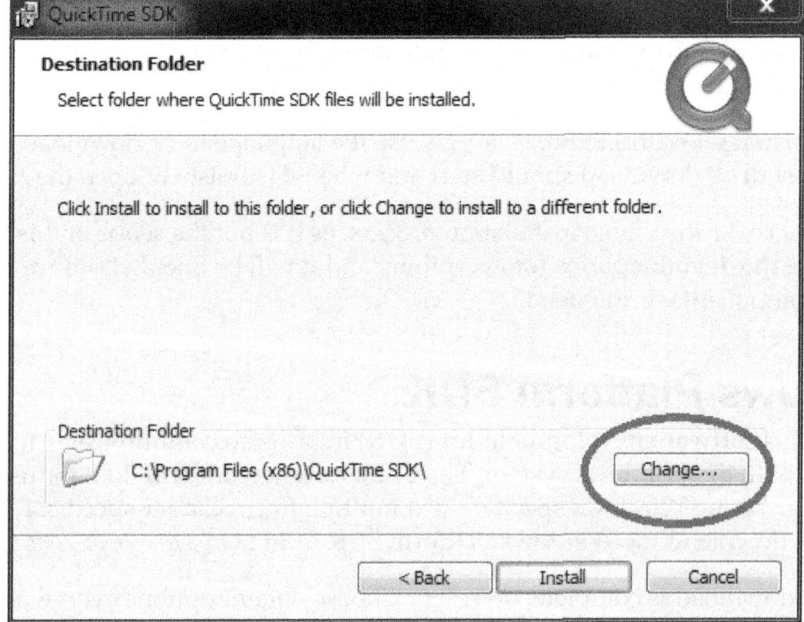

Now change the **Destination Folder** path to `C:\QuickTimeSDK-7.3`.

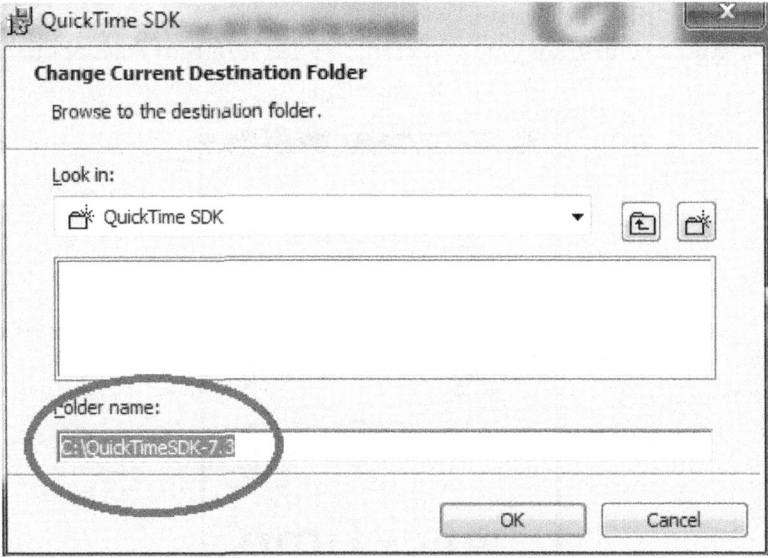

If you are familiar with the re-linking libraries, do not bother yourself with this warning.

Launching the sample application

Before launching your first sample application, make sure that you have QuickTime Player installed on your system. If not, go to `http://www.apple.com/quicktime/download/`, download, and install it.

Go to the Cinder samples directory, for example, `C:/cinder/samples/` and find a folder with the name QuickTime. Open `C:/cinder/samples/QuickTime/vc10/quickTimeSample.sln`.

>
> **Downloading the color images of this book**
>
> We also provide you a PDF file that has color images of the screenshots/diagrams used in this book. The color images will help you better understand the changes in the output.
>
> You can download this file from:
>
> `http://www.packtpub.com/sites/default/files/downloads/9564OS_ColoredImages.pdf`

Learn Cinder Basics – Now!

Welcome to Microsoft Visual C++ 2010! Press *F5* to build a project and run it. You should be provided with a prompt to choose a file—select a QuickTime compatible movie file from your hard drive and see what happens. You should see the movie playing back, and a semi-transparent rectangle with different stats about the movie file over it.

If you don't see the movie, check if you have QuickTime Player installed. First time I tried this sample application, I didn't succeed. And I spent hours trying to understand, what's wrong? Nothing! You just don' t have QuickTime Player. Get it from `http://www.apple.com/quicktime/download/`.

Summary

To sum up, these are the most simplest and fastest ways you can get Cinder up and running. There are other possible ways too, but they are out of the scope of t his book. But if you search for the latest version of Cinder, check the *CINDER + GIT* section on the Cinder official website (`http://libcinder.org/docs/welcome/GitSetup.html`).

In the next chapter, we will try to understand what is possible with Cinder by launching different samples in the Cinder samples package.

2
Know What is Possible – The Cinder Toolset

This chapter introduces various basic tasks that can be performed with Cinder through compiling, running, changing, and discussing some of the sample applications.

We have already tested our setup by compiling and running the QuickTime sample application. Now, we are going to see what is possible with Cinder by compiling other samples and discussing what is so special about them.

We will go through samples that show most of the functionalities that will be discussed throughout this book. There will be many parts that are not clear and not easy to explain yet, but do not worry, we will try to understand them during the following chapters.

Here is a list of some of the examples that we are going to discuss. Go to your Cinder samples folder (`/Users/You/cinder/samples/` on Mac OS X and `C:\cinder\samples\` on Windows, if you have followed the tutorial in the previous chapter).

- BasicApp (`samples/basicApp`)
- BezierPath (`samples/bezierPath`)
- CairoBasic (`samples/CairoBasic`)
- CaptureTest (`samples/captureTest`)
- EaseGallery (`samples/EaseGallery`)
- TextBox (`samples/TextBox`)
- ArcballDemo (`samples/ArcballDemo`)
- Earthquake (`samples/Earthquake`)
- AudioGenerative (`samples/AudioGenerative`)

BasicApp

Go to your Cinder samples folder (`/Users/You/cinder/samples/` on MAC and `C:\cinder\samples\` on Windows, if you have followed the tutorial in the previous chapter).

There will be a folder with the name `BasicApp`. Take a look at what's there inside. If you are a Mac OS X user, open the project file at `xcode/basicApp.xcodeproj`. Windows users should open the project file from `vc10\basicApp.sln`. Compile and run the project.

As we can see, a window with a black background appears. It seems that there is nothing there except pure blackness and an infinite void. But that's not true! Grab your mouse and try to fill the void by pointing and clicking-and-dragging anywhere on the black surface of the application window. An Orange line appears. Yes, it is a very basic drawing program that allows you to draw a continuous line. Line is one of the basic 2D geometric shapes that can be created with Cinder.

Let's try to change the color of the line. Close the window and click on the `basicApp.cpp` file located in the Source directory of the sample project found in the project navigator or project file tree browser of the chosen IDE. Navigate to a place in the code where you can see the following:

```
void BasicApp::draw()
{
```

This is the place where the actual drawing procedures of the program are defined. Go to the following lines of code:

```
// We'll set the color to orange
glColor3f( 1.0f, 0.5f, 0.25f );
```

This is the place where the color of the line can be changed. It is done by using a function called `glColor3f`. From the name of the function it is possible to tell that it uses OpenGL, changes color, and uses three `float` values for that. It is known that RGB color values consist of three components that are R (red), G (green), and B (blue). In this function, `0.0` is the minimal possible value for each component and `1.0` is the maximum.

Let's change the color of the line to red. We will need to set the red component of the color to maximum (`1.0`) and all others to minimum (`0.0`). So it will look like the following:

```
glColor3f( 1.0f, 0.0f, 0.0f );
```

The reason why we use the *dot-zero-f* notation is that we want to tell the compiler that we are passing floating-point constants to the function. I will not dig into this here, as there are a lot of online resources about that on the Internet.

Now save, compile, run, and draw. Well done! You made your first custom line of code with Cinder! Let's continue with another example right away!

BezierPath

Now, we are ready for a little bit more of a complicated example that will allow you to draw a continuous Bézier curve. Bézier curves are called so because of a french engineer Pierre Bézier who actually patented and made them popular by applying them in designs. Bézier curves are widely used in computer graphics, animations, and other fields. The concept of Bézier curves allows us to create parametric curved lines by using the Cartesian coordinate system and numbers.

Go to your Cinder samples folder (`/Users/You/cinder/samples/` on Mac OS X and `C:\cinder\samples\` if you use Windows).

Know What is Possible – The Cinder Toolset

Go to the folder named `bezierPath`. Open `xcode/bezierPath.xcodeproj`, if you are a Mac OS X user (`vc10\bezierPath.sln`, if you are using Windows). Compile and run the project.

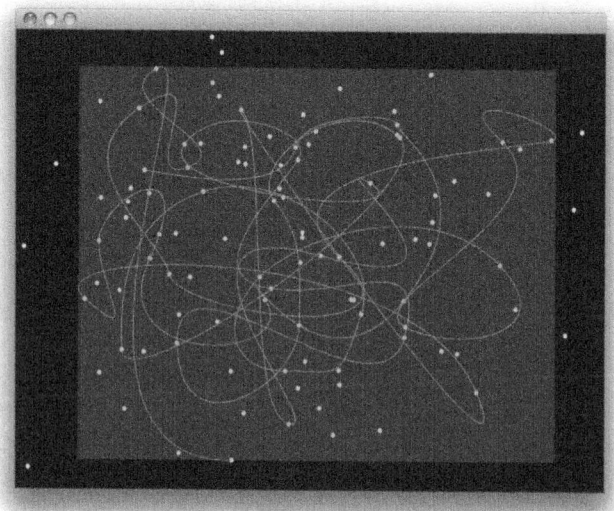

Click-and-drag to place points on the surface of the window. You will start to see the line after the second click. By moving the mouse while you hold it down, you can control the curvature of the line segment that is being drawn. Play around a bit to get a better understanding about how Bézier curves work.

To add some extra geek-fun to the process, let's change something as we did in the previous example. Close the application window and open the file `bezierPathApp.cpp` in the editor. Let's assume that we don't like the circles that are drawn on the screen to indicate the points that form the path—we want to draw rectangles instead. Navigate to a block of code that looks like the following code snippet:

```
// draw the control points
gl::color( Color( 1.0f, 1.0f, 0.0f ) );
for( size_t p = 0; p < mPath.getNumPoints(); ++p )
    gl::drawSolidCircle( mPath.getPoint( p ), 2.5f );
```

As you can see in the comment in the preceding block, this block is responsible for drawing the control points. It sets the color of the next thing to be drawn (or circle in this case) with the help of the following line:

```
gl::color( Color( 1.0f, 1.0f, 0.0f ) );
```

Chapter 2

This uses a `for` loop to iterate through all the data in the `mPath` object. Circles are drawn with the help of the following line:

```
gl::drawSolidCircle( mPath.getPoint( p ), 2.5f );
```

Just by looking at the function name we can tell that it draws circles. `gl::` tells us that this function resides in the Cinder OpenGL namespace (Cinder uses namespaces a lot, and that makes its code more readable indeed), `draw` tells us that it draws something, `solid` means that this function draws something solid, and `circle` concludes this by making it clear that with the help of OpenGL a solid circle will be drawn.

Two parameters are passed to the function. The first one is a point object that holds x and y coordinate values and the other one defines the radius of the circle being drawn in pixels.

Let's start by changing the radius of the circle. Change `2.5f` to `10.0f` so that it looks like the following:

```
gl::drawSolidCircle( mPath.getPoint( p ), 10.0f );
```

Build and run the project to see the change! Hmm, interesting! It is indeed! But let's not celebrate yet, remember, we wanted to change the circle into a rectangle. We will use a function defined as follows:

```
gl::drawSolidRect( const Rectf &rect, bool textureRectangle=false );
```

As the name of the function tells us, this function draws a solid rectangle. We have to provide a parameter to the function though. Just one parameter is required (the other one is optional and set to `false` by default) and that has to be of the type `Rectf`. A `Rectf` consisting of four values. The first two values define the upper-right corner of the rectangle and the other two define the location of the bottom-right corner. It is a bit different in most drawing APIs, as usually this kind of object is defined by passing in the x and y coordinates of the top-left corner and the width and height of the rectangle. Not this time. So we have to pass something like the following:

```
Rectf( float x1, float y1, float x2, float y2 )
```

Where `x1` is the x coordinate of the top-left corner, `y1` is the y coordinate of the top-left corner, and `x2` and `y2` define where the bottom-right corner should be on the screen.

This is just one of the five `Rectf` (or `RectT`) constructors in Cinder. If you want to see other ones, take a look in the Cinder online reference at http://libcinder.org/docs/v0.8.4/classcinder_1_1_rect_t.html.

[19]

Know What is Possible – The Cinder Toolset

By analyzing the point drawing function (`gl::drawSolidCircle( mPath.getPoint( p ), 10.0f );`), we get a piece of code that represents an object that holds the x and y coordinates of the current control point:

```
mPath.getPoint(p)
```

We can access the x and y coordinates by writing:

```
mPath.getPoint(p).x
```

And

```
mPath.getPoint(p).y
```

Let's construct our rectangle:

```
Rectf( mPath.getPoint(p).x, mPath.getPoint(p).y,
   mPath.getPoint(p).x+10.0f, mPath.getPoint(p).y+10.0f )
```

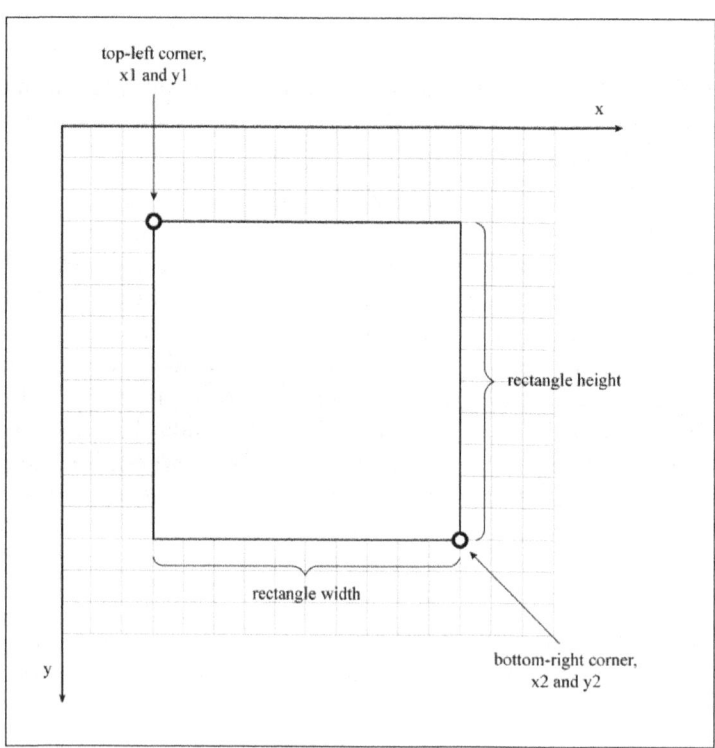

The number constant `10.0f` in the preceding piece of code represents the width and height of the rectangle. As we want the width and height to be equal, we use equal values here. The following is the final code:

```
// draw the control points
gl::color( Color( 1.0f, 1.0f, 0.0f ) );
for( size_t p = 0; p < mPath.getNumPoints(); ++p ) {
  gl::drawSolidRect( Rectf( mPath.getPoint(p).x,
    mPath.getPoint(p).y, mPath.getPoint(p).x+10.0f,
    mPath.getPoint(p).y+10.0f ) );
}
```

Build and run the project. What you will see is that rectangles are drawn next to the actual control points, not on them as it should be. Let's fix that:

```
for( size_t p = 0; p < mPath.getNumPoints(); ++p ) {
  gl::drawSolidRect( Rectf( mPath.getPoint(p).x-5.0f,
    mPath.getPoint(p).y-5.0f, mPath.getPoint(p).x+5.0f,
    mPath.getPoint(p).y+5.0f ) );
}
```

As you can see, we changed all the `10.0f'` values to `5.0f` and subtracted `5.0f` from the first two parameters of the rectangle constructor. By doing that we moved the top-left corner of the rectangle to left by the half of its width and up by the half of its height (5 pixels), while keeping the same width and height (10 pixels).

Build and run the project, and as you can see, now the rectangle is in its right place.

Maybe this is a bit too complicated in the beginning, but the more you do these kind of adjustments the more you learn. We won't be making any more changes during the rest of this chapter.

CairoBasic

Have you ever dreamt of creating generative print artwork that could be printed in any size without losing quality? Meet Cairo.

Cairo is a vector-graphics software library that allows you to draw all the crazy vector stuff that can be done in software, such as Illustrator, and it allows us to save it as a separate vector-graphics file. If you want to know more about Cairo itself, visit it website (http://cairographics.org/).

Know What is Possible – The Cinder Toolset

Let's try this out! Search for the `CairoBasic` folder in the `samples` directory. Open `xcode/CairoBasic.xcodeproj` (`vc10\CairoBasic.sln`, if you're on Windows). Build and run the project. Nothing special seems to be there except a radial gradient background. But try to click on it! A flower. Click again! Random flowers. Try to fill the entire screen with them—you can smell the aroma, right?

Ok, that's enough. Close the application window. So, what did just happen? To understand this open the file `CairoBasicApp.cpp` in your code editor. I won't explain it yet, but it is possible to see that there is not very much code in it. Go to a block of code that looks like the following:

```
void CairoBasicApp::keyDown( KeyEvent event )
{
```

This is a method of the main application class that does something when we press a key on the keyboard. We can see that it is possible to make the application fullscreen, if we press *F*, and then there is something defined for letters *S*, *E*, *P*, and *D*—what is it? If you press one of these buttons, you save the ready image in a file, but the file format of this file will be a vector one. As you can see, if you press *S*, you get a SVG file, for *E* you get an EPS, for *P* you get a PS or PostScript file, and for *D* you get a PDF.

Try it out! Build and run the application again, create your artwork, and press *S*, *E*, *P*, and *D* one after another. Then go to your home folder (`/Users/You/` on MAC and `C:\Users\You` on Windows) and you will see that there are four new files:

- `CairoBasicShot.svg`
- `CairoBasicShot.eps`

- `CairoBasicShot.ps`
- `CairoBasicShot.pdf`

Try to open one of these files with your favorite vector-graphics software.

 You can open the `CairoBasicShot.svg` file with your web browser as well. That means you do not need to convert vector-graphics to a format such as JPG or PNG, if you want to use it on the web—you can use it in the SVG vector file format right away.

Yes, it is true, you can zoom in to infinity and the details remain crisp and clear. That is the power of vector-graphics! Now you can post-process and print that 1 m x 1 m generative flower poster in 300 dpi without losing any detail. Cool, isn't it? And you can do so much more except just printing your artwork—you can use it as a base for physical objects to be made with a laser cutter or a CNC mill, for example.

CaptureTest

In the first chapter, we saw that Cinder is capable of loading and playing back video files. So, how about using real-time footage? This sample application shows that it is possible to access video from a webcam that is connected to your computer.

Go search for a folder called `captureTest` (`CaptureBasic` in Cinder 0.8.5) in the `samples` directory. Open `xcode/captureTest.xcodeproj` (`vc10\captureTest.sln`, if you're using Windows). Build and run the project. Wait a bit, you should see the moving image from your camera.

There is nothing much more about this sample, it just captures and displays the image of the webcam. You can use this real-time data in many different ways later.

[23]

EaseGallery

As we are going to do some animation with Cinder, it would be nice to just see some of the possibilities Cinder provides us for that. Go on and open up the folder named `EaseGallery` in the `samples` directory. Open `xcode/EaseGallery.xcodeproj` (`vc10\EaseGallery.sln`, if you are a Windows user). Build and run the project.

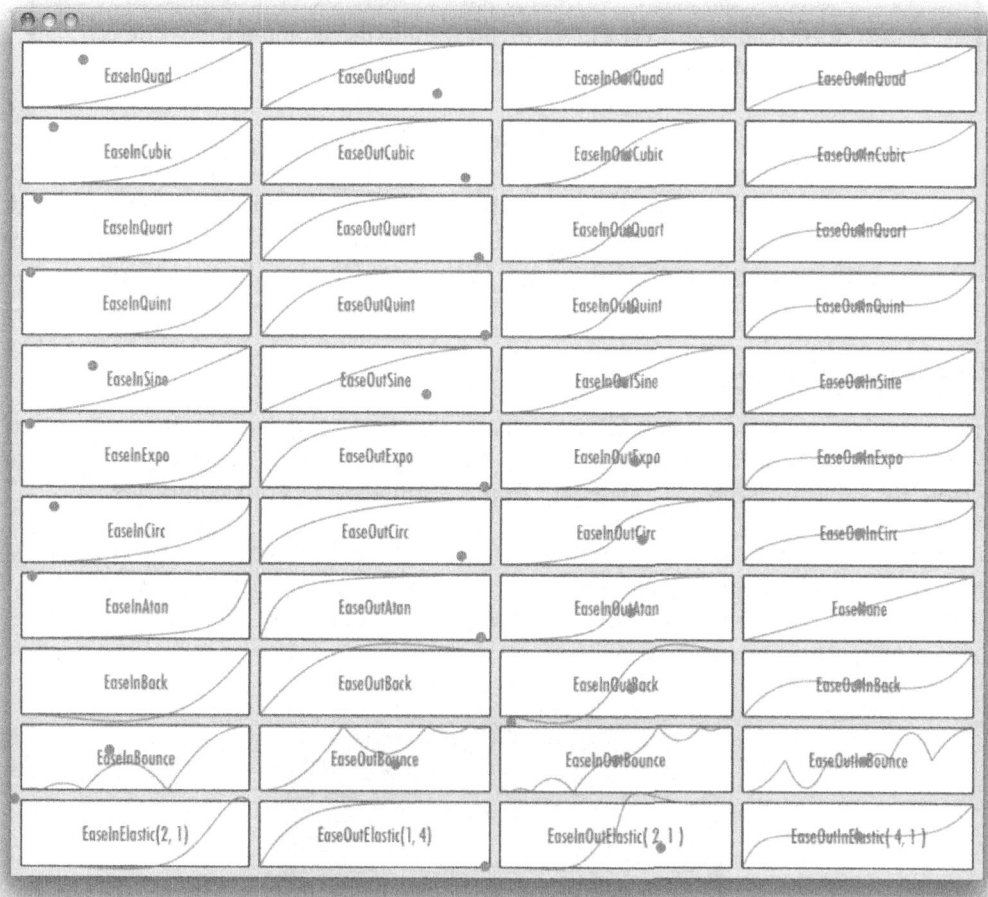

If you are familiar with some kind of animation software or the TweenLite ActionScript library, you might remember a term called *easing*. This is what the EaseGallery example is about. Here you can see all the different animation easing algorithms that Cinder provides. We will dig a bit deeper into this later, but for now you just have to remember that there are such functions and you won't have to search for them in the darkest places of the Internet or implement them by yourself.

TextBox

Cinder has a very good text support—even for those whose native language alphabets consist of non-English alphabet characters.

Let's search for a folder named `TextBox` in the `samples` directory. Open `xcode/TextBox.xcodeproj` (`vc10\TextBox.sln`, if you are a Windows user). Build and run the project. Click anywhere in the window. When you click-and-drag, the text box changes its width. Even more, the text inside it wraps accordingly. A rectangle that represents the full width and height of the space the text occupies is being drawn behind it.

Let's close the window and try to make some changes (yes I lied, we are making changes again) to the application. Open `TextBoxApp.cpp` and find a block of code that looks like the following:

```
void TextBoxApp::render()
{
  string txt = "Here is some text that is larger than can fit
  naturally inside of 100 pixels.\nAnd here is another line after
  a hard break.";
```

Try to change the text within the quotes (don't be afraid to use unicode characters):

```
string txt = "Hi, that's me, Ratman!\nWhere is Mickey Mouse?";
```

Save the file, and build and run the project again. If you used unicode characters, you will be positively surprised—all the characters are there!

[25]

ArcballDemo

This sample demonstrates the basic 3D capabilities of Cinder. Go to the `ArcballDemo` directory in the `samples` folder and open `xcode/ArcballDemo.xcodeproj` (`vc10\ArcBallDemo.sln`, if you are using Windows).

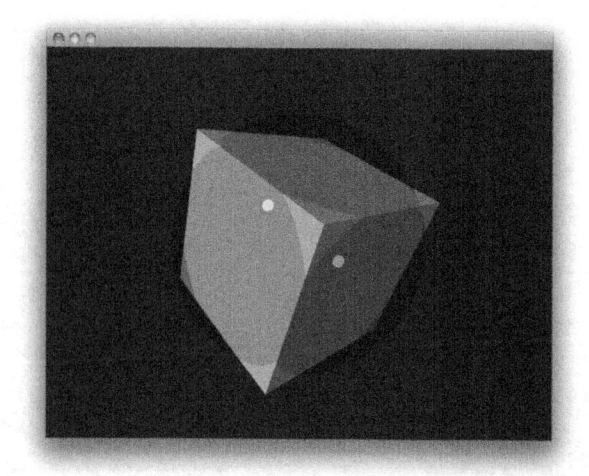

A strange image appears within the application window. Don't worry, just click-and-drag. You will notice that it is a 3D cube. I won't explain other things that were meant to demonstrate through this demo, but the important thing to know is that rendering (of the default Open GL render mode) in Cinder is done by using Open GL and that means that you can render 2D images, as well as 3D space.

Earthquake

If you open up this example, you will see how much detail you can get with real-time 3D graphics in Cinder. Find the `Earthquake` directory in the `samples` folder, open `xcode/Earthquake.xcodeproj` (`vc10\Earthquake.sln`, if you are using Windows). Build and run the application.

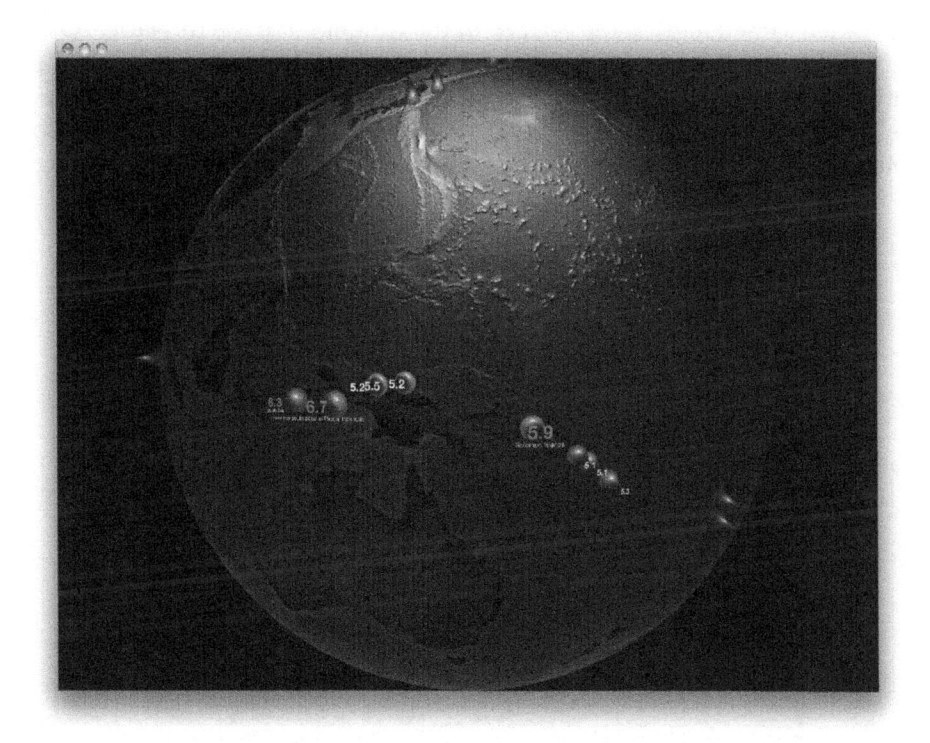

What you should see is a 3D model of the earth and red cones with numbers on them. You can rotate it by moving your mouse and zooming in and out by using your mousewheel.

Real-time interactive 3D application, isn't it awesome?

AudioGenerative

Welcome to the world of generative audio! This application sample will show you some possibilities of real-time audio-visual world.

Find the folder named `AudioGenerative` in the Cinder `samples` directory. Open up the project file `xcode/AudioGenerative.xcodeproj` (`vc10\AudioGenerative.sln`, if you are using Windows). Build and run the application. Turn up the volume, but don't be afraid! It's just a sine wave. Try to move your mouse up and down above the application window—you will change the frequency of the sound by doing that.

Summary

So we went through just a couple of samples that are included in the Cinder samples package. There are more, and one of the best ways you can learn about Cinder is to go through all the examples, try to change some parts of them, and try to understand how that works.

The discussion about the examples here was meant to be as an intro to the Cinder features that will be discussed in the next chapters. I recommend trying to compile and run all the samples so that you get as broad understanding about Cinder features as possible.

3
Initial Setup – Creating the BaseApp

In this chapter, we are going to create a Hello World application from scratch. The application will be called BaseApp and we will use it's structure as a starting point in further chapters.

This chapter will cover the following:

- Setting up a project with TinderBox
- Setting up a project from scratch on Mac OS X (Xcode 3 and 4+)
- Setting up a project from scratch on Windows

It does not have much in common with the BasicApp from the previous chapter except the basic structure, which will be common to all Cinder projects.

TinderBox

The easiest way to create a Cinder project is to use its integrated tool called **TinderBox**. You can find it in the `cinder/tools/` directory. This will work with both Mac OS X and Windows.

Initial Setup – Creating the BaseApp

Let's give it a try. Open TinderBox application. If you are doing it for the first time, you will have to point to your Cinder directory.

When you've done that, the TinderBox project setup window will appear. Choose **Basic App** from the **Target** and **OpenGL** from the **Template** drop-down lists. Enter BaseApp in the **Project Name** field. Make sure that you have **Base** in the **Naming Prefix** field.

> For those who use Cinder 0.8.5, there is no **Target** list in the new TinderBox. You have to choose the **Basic OpenGL** template. Also, there is no **Naming Prefix** field in the new TinderBox, so just ignore it.

Choose a directory where you will store your Cinder projects in the **Location** field. Mine is /Users/kr15h/Documents/CinderProjects/ (C:\Users\kr15h\Documents\CinderProjects\ on Windows).

Leave **HEAD** in the **Cinder Version** field and choose **Xcode** in the **Compilers** section. Choose **Visual C++ 2010** if you're using Windows or both if you plan to develop using both operating systems.

Click on **Create**!

Your project is ready! Navigate to your Cinder project's folder that you specified in the **Location** field and you'll find a folder called `BaseApp` there. You will find an Xcode project file in the `xcode` directory (Visual C++ 2010 project file in the `vc10` directory on Windows).

Open `BaseApp.xcodeproj` (`BaseApp.sln` on Windows).

Try to build and run it. You should see the output as shown in the following screenshot:

Nothing interesting is drawn in the window yet. We will make some changes a bit later, but if you are able to compile, run, and see this, you are the master!

Creating a project from scratch (Mac OS X)

Some of us just want to do it the difficult way, which is not so difficult actually, but involves certain steps that have to be remembered and understood. What if there was no TinderBox? No problem!

Here we will split up in two groups again—this time depending on the version of Xcode we are using. There is the old way (Xcode 3) and the new way (Xcode 4+). You can check the version by opening the Xcode and selecting **AboutXcode** from the **Xcode** menu.

> If you are using Cinder 0.8.5, be aware of the fact that the minimum required Mac OS X version is 10.7 and you do need Xcode 4.4+.

Initial Setup – Creating the BaseApp

Basic project setup (Xcode 3)

Go to your Cinder project's directory, which in my case is `/Users/kr15h/Documents/CinderProjects/`. Create an empty directory for our new project and name it `BaseApp`. Create another directory inside it and call it `src`. It should look like the one shown in the following screenshot:

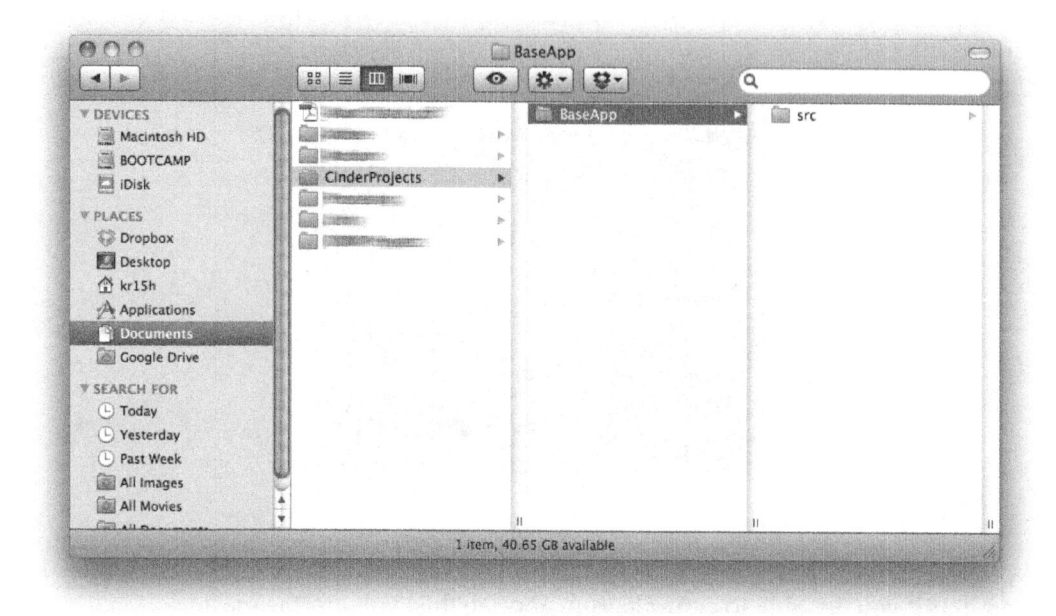

Open up the Xcode and select **New Project** from the **File** menu. Select the **Mac OS X Application** category and choose **Cocoa Application**. Click on **Choose**, browse to the directory we created earlier (`CinderProjects/BaseApp`), and then click on **Save**.

Now it is recommended to close the Xcode, browse to your newly created project directory, and rename the Xcode project folder (`BaseApp` inside BaseApp—the one that is parent to the .xcodeproj file) to `xcode`.

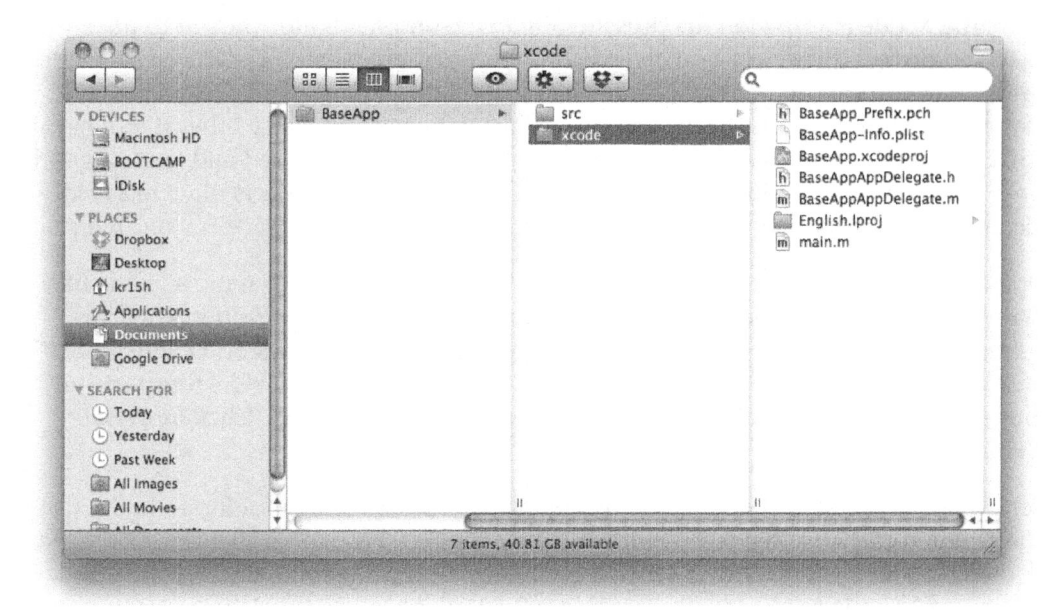

Now open up the `BaseApp.xcodeproj` file. We have to remove some files that we won't need. These files include `main.m`, `InfoPlist.strings`, `MainMenu.xib` as well as `BaseAppAppDelegate.m` and `BaseAppAppDelegate.h`. Click on **Also Move to Trash** when prompted.

Let's create our first source file. Right-click on the **Classes** folder in the **Xcode Project Navigator** pane and select **Add | New File**. Choose **C++ File** from the **C and C++** category. Name it `BaseApp` and uncheck the **Also create "BaseApp.h"** option. For the location, choose the `BaseApp/src` folder that we created earlier and click on **Finish**.

Basic project setup (Xcode 4+)

Open up Xcode and select **New | New Project** from the **File** menu. Select the **Application** item under the **Mac OS X** category and choose **Cocoa Application**. Click on **Next**. Enter `BaseApp` as **Product Name** and something, for example, `com.mycompany` as **Company Identifier**. Click on **Next** again and you will be prompted to choose the location for your project. Browse to the directory we created earlier (`CinderProjects/BaseApp`) and click on **Create**.

Initial Setup – Creating the BaseApp

Close the Xcode (completely by pressing *Cmd + Q*) and navigate yourself to the BaseApp project directory. You can see two folders there, `BaseApp` and `src`. Rename `BaseApp` to `xcode`—all the Xcode-relevant stuff will be stored there and all the code that will be stored in the `src` directory is meant to be used in every other IDE. This is not a law, it is just how Cinder sample projects are being organized and that's a good way of keeping a cross-platform code project well organized. This is done to avoid the need to create a separate version of the source files for each platform and IDE.

Open the `BaseApp.xcodeproj` Xcode project file. We are going to remove some files that we won't need. In the Project Navigator, under the **BaseApp** folder, select and delete `AppDelegate.h`, `AppDelegate.m`, and `MainMenu.xib`. Click on **Delete** when prompted to remove the actual files, not just the references. Under the **Supporting files** folder, select and remove `main.m` and `BaseApp-Prefix.pch`. Click on **Delete** again when prompted.

Let's create our first C++ source file. Right-click on the **BaseApp** folder in the Project Navigator and choose the **New File** option. Select **C++ File** under the **Mac OS X** and **C and C++** categories. A **Save As** dialog will appear. Navigate to the `src` directory of our `BaseApp` project (`BaseApp/src`). Name the file as `BaseApp` and click on **Create**.

Adding code (Xcode 3 and 4+)

Open the file we just created (`BaseApp.cpp`) in the editor and enter the following piece of code:

```
#include "cinder/app/AppBasic.h"
#include "cinder/gl/gl.h"

using namespace ci;
using namespace ci::app;
using namespace std;

class BaseApp : public AppBasic {
public:
  void setup();
  void update();
  void draw();
};

void BaseApp::setup(){}
void BaseApp::update(){}
```

```
void BaseApp::draw()
{
  // clear out the window with black
  gl::clear( Color( 0, 0, 0 ) );
}

CINDER_APP_BASIC( BaseApp, RendererGl )
```

If you try to compile and run the application, you will see that it is not possible. Some things are still missing and those are the connections with Cinder libraries and headers.

Connecting to Cinder (Xcode 3)

Under the **Project** menu, select **Edit Project Settings**. Go to the **Build** tab and in the **Configuration** select field, choose **All Configurations**. Let's add a user-defined build setting that will prove itself useful in a moment. This user-defined setting will store the location of the Cinder directory relative to our project. Click on the little gear button at the bottom-left corner of the **Project Settings** window and choose **Add User-Defined Setting**.

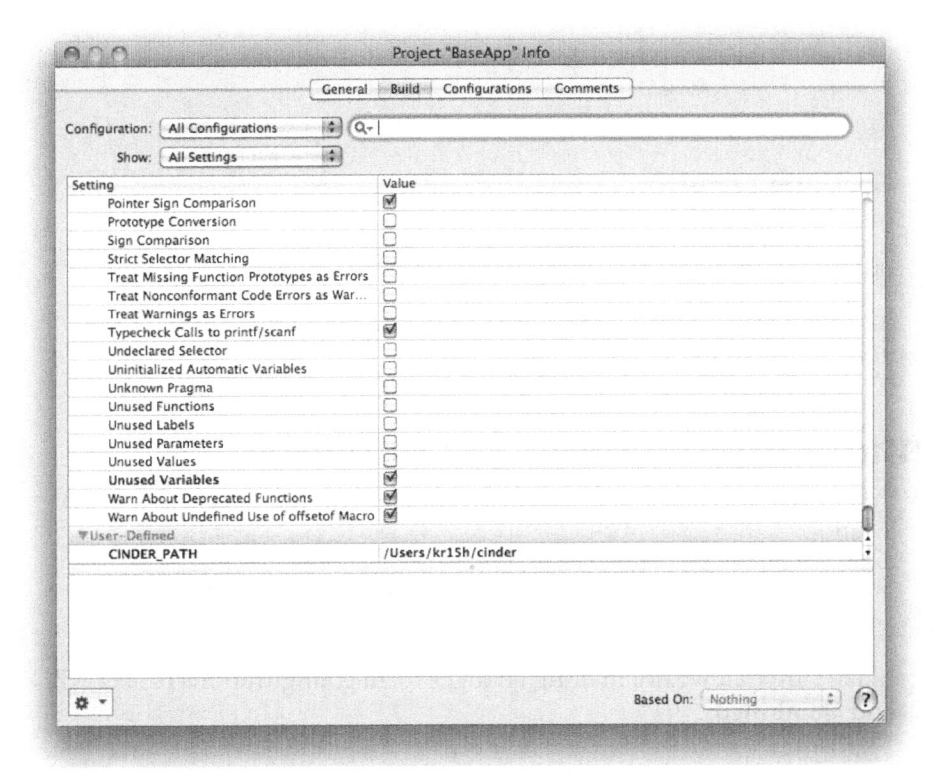

Initial Setup – Creating the BaseApp

Name it as `CINDER_PATH` and set the value to the location of Cinder directory / `Users/You/cinder` (replace `You` with your username).

Now we have to make use of this newly created variable. Scroll to the **Search Paths** section and modify the **User Header Search Paths** setting. Set the value to `$(CINDER_PATH)/include`. With that done, go to **Header Search Paths** (notice that there is no user in front of it) and set it to `$(CINDER_PATH)/boost`.

Then go to the **Architectures** section and set the **Architectures** variable to `i386`.

Next, we have to tell Xcode where to find Cinder libraries for linking. Find the **Linking** section and change the **Debug** field under **Other Linker Flags** to `$(CINDER_PATH)/lib/libcinder_d.a` and the **Release** field to `$(CINDER_PATH)/lib/libcinder.a`.

Now for the final thing. We need to add Mac OS X frameworks that are needed for our Cinder applications. Close the **Project Settings** panel and right-click on the **Frameworks** folder in the Xcode Project Navigator and go to **Add | Existing Frameworks**. Then, select the following:

- `Accelerate.framework`
- `AudioToolbox.framework`
- `AudioUnit.framework`
- `CoreAudio.framework`
- `CoreVideo.framework`
- `OpenGL.framework`
- `QTKit.framework`
- `QuickTime.framework`

Compile and run the project. Success! Now, you are ready to go to the *Final Adjustments* section of this chapter.

Connecting to Cinder (Xcode 4+)

Follow these steps to create a user-defined variable with the path to our main Cinder location:

1. Select the **BaseApp** project icon in the Xcode Project Navigator pane.
2. Choose the **BaseApp** target under the **Targets** category.
3. Make sure that we are making changes to all configurations (select **All** and **Combined**).

4. Click on the **Add Build Setting** button and select **Add User-Defined Setting** from the menu.

5. Call it `CINDER_PATH` and enter the path to the place you copied your Cinder files.

Now we have to make use of this newly created variable. Scroll to the **Search Paths** section and modify the **User Header Search Paths** setting. Set the value to `$(CINDER_PATH)/include`. With that done, go to **Header Search Paths** (notice that there is no user in front of it) and set it to `$(CINDER_PATH)/boost`.

Then go to the **Architectures** section and set the **Architectures** variable to `i386`.

Next, we have to tell Xcode where to find Cinder libraries for linking. Find the **Linking** section, and change the **Debug** field under **Other Linker Flags** to `$(CINDER_PATH)/lib/libcinder_d.a` and the **Release** field to `$(CINDER_PATH)/lib/libcinder.a`.

There is another thing that Xcode added automatically for us, a link to the prefix header file that we deleted earlier. This will throw an error while compiling because the compiler won't be able to find the prefix header file. Go to the **Apple LLVM compiler 3.0 – Language** tab and clear out the **Prefix Header** field for both **Debug** and **Release**.

Initial Setup – Creating the BaseApp

Finally, we have to link our application to the Mac OS X framework libraries. To do that, follow these steps:

1. Go to the **Build Phases** tab.
2. Expand the **Link Binary With Libraries** section.
3. Click on the **Add Items** button to choose frameworks.

Select the following frameworks and click on **Add**:

- `Accelerate.framework`
- `AudioToolbox.framework`
- `AudioUnit.framework`
- `CoreAudio.framework`
- `CoreVideo.framework`
- `OpenGL.framework`
- `QTKit.framework`
- `QuickTime.framework`

That's it! Compile and run the project. Success! Now, you are ready to go to the **Final Adjustments** section of this chapter.

Creating a project from scratch (Windows)

So you are on Windows, right? Let's create an empty project in Visual C++. We will link it to all the necessary libraries and make sure that it is possible to compile the project before we move on.

Go to your Cinder project directory (which in my case is `C:\Users\kr15h\Documents\CinderProjects\`) and create a new directory `BaseApp` there.

Open Microsoft Visual C++ 2010 and go to **File | New | Project**. Choose **Win32 Project** from the **Win32** category. Enter the name `BaseApp` in the **Name** field and your BaseApp project directory that we just created in the **Location** field. Make sure that the **Create directory for solution** checkbox is not checked and the solution name is `BaseApp`—the same as the name of the project.

In the **Application Settings** dialog, check the **Empty project** checkbox and make sure that you choose **Windows application** as the **Application** type. Click on **Finish**.

Close Visual C++ and go to the `BaseApp` project directory. You will see another directory with a name `BaseApp` inside it—rename it to `vc10`.

Create a new directory in the same level where the `vc10` folder is and rename it to `src`. Open the `BaseApp.sln` file in the `vc10` folder. Create a new C++ file. Choose **File | New File**. In the dialog box, choose the **Visual C++** template category and select **C++ File**. Click on **Open**. A blank file will open in the editor. Enter the following piece of code there:

```cpp
#include "cinder/app/AppBasic.h"
#include "cinder/gl/gl.h"

using namespace ci;
using namespace ci::app;
using namespace std;

class BaseApp : public AppBasic {
public:
  void setup();
  void update();
  void draw();
};
```

Initial Setup – Creating the BaseApp

```
void BaseApp::setup(){}
void BaseApp::update(){}

void BaseApp::draw()
{
  // clear out the window with black
  gl::clear( Color( 0, 0, 0 ) );
}

CINDER_APP_BASIC( BaseApp, RendererGl )
```

Go to **File | Save As**, navigate to the `BaseApp\src` directory, and save the file with the name `BaseApp.cpp`. To keep things organized, navigate to the **BaseApp** folder in the Explorer and click-and-drag it to the **Source Files** directory in the Visual C++ 2010 Solution Explorer.

You won't be able to compile and run it yet. There are some more things to do.

Go to **Project | BaseApp Properties**. Choose **All Configurations** in the **Configurations** select field.

Click on the **C/C++** category in the left column and find the **Additional Include Directories** field in the right column. Add the following paths there:

- `C:\cinder\include`
- `C:\cinder\boost`

Click on **Linker** in the left column and edit value of the **Additional Library Directories** field. You have to enter the following two paths there:

- `C:\cinder\lib`
- `C:\cinder\lib\msw`

Click on **OK**. Now select the **Debug** configuration and click on **Input** under **Linker** in the left column of the **Project Properties** window. Add `cinder_d.lib` to the **Additional Dependencies** field and `LIBCMT` in the **Ignore Specific Default Libraries** field.

With that done, select the **Release** configuration and add `cinder.lib` to the **Additional Dependencies** field.

Click on **OK**. Build and run the application. A window with a black background should appear. If so, you are the master and we may continue with the next section.

Final adjustments

No matter what kind of setup you choose, you'll have to edit one single file that is located in the same place relative to the project directory and whose name is the same in all configurations, `src/BaseApp.cpp`. Open it. We will try to understand what the different lines of code mean.

```
#include "cinder/app/AppBasic.h"
#include "cinder/gl/gl.h"
```

These are the initial `include` statements that are responsible for including all the necessary Cinder stuff before we start to write our actual Cinder code.

```
using namespace ci;
using namespace ci::app;
using namespace std;
```

Here we tell the compiler that we are going to use some namespaces. We do that to avoid writing the namespace names before the variables and methods that are defined in those namespaces in our code. So, these lines are here just to make our code more readable and our creative lives easier. We are not adding the `gl` namespace here, because we want to keep the OpenGL drawing code distinguishable from all other code in the file.

```
class BaseApp : public AppBasic {
```

This is the definition of our base application class. It extends Cinder AppBasic—it is a super class that contains all the basic functionality that we would need to code ourselves if there was no Cinder.

```
void setup();
void update();
void draw();
```

These are the methods that we are going to override in this class. These methods can be considered the most important in Cinder, because here you can define what will be done in the main run loop of the program.

`setup()` is for setting up your program and it is executed just once at the beginning.

`update()` is called for every frame before the `draw()` function (the default Cinder frame rate is 30 fps) and here you should put all your calculations, data retrieval, and analysis code.

Initial Setup – Creating the BaseApp

`draw()` is for drawing things on the screen. As `update()` takes care of all the calculations, you can use the results here in order to draw something on the screen. It can be 2D or 3D text, 2D or 3D shapes—a certain point in a movie file. Choose whatever you want, but try to use this method just for drawing.

Then there are implementations of the methods (after the class declaration that starts with the class `BaseApp : public AppBasic {` and ends with a closing bracket `}`) and a line of code that is responsible for launching your program is as follows:

```
CINDER_APP_BASIC( BaseApp, RendererGl )
```

This tells Cinder that it has to run your program (`BaseApp`) with the help of `RendererGl`. `RendererGl`, one of the available renderers in Cinder. It uses OpenGL for rendering and that lets you use the classes and functions defined in the `gl::` namespace as well as pure OpenGL functions.

There are some other renderers available in Cinder, for example, `Renderer2d` that can be used in combination with Cairo vector-graphics Cinder namespace. It uses the `Cairo::createWindowSurface()` function for drawing and it may be not so fast as when using OpenGL.

OK, now we are ready to add some visual feedback to our program. We do it inside the implementation of the `draw()` method.

Let's draw some lines. Edit the `draw()` method implementation as follows:

```
void BaseApp::draw()
{
  // clear out the window with black
  gl::clear( Color( 0.0f, 0.0f, 0.0f ) );
```

Before we begin writing the actual drawing code, let me explain to you the difference between Cinder and OpenGL coordinate space.

In Cinder (as in many other creative coding frameworks and 2D graphics software), we make use of the so called fourth quadrant of the 2D Cartesian coordinate system. That means that the point (0, 0) is located at the top-left corner of the screen. To the right from that point all the x values go positive, and downwards from it all the y values go positive.

It is different with OpenGL. All four quadrants are used and the point (0, 0) is located in the center of the screen. You might remember this from math classes at school—to the left from the (0, 0) point x values go negative, to the right they go positive. Downwards from the (0, 0) point, the y values go negative, and upwards they go positive.

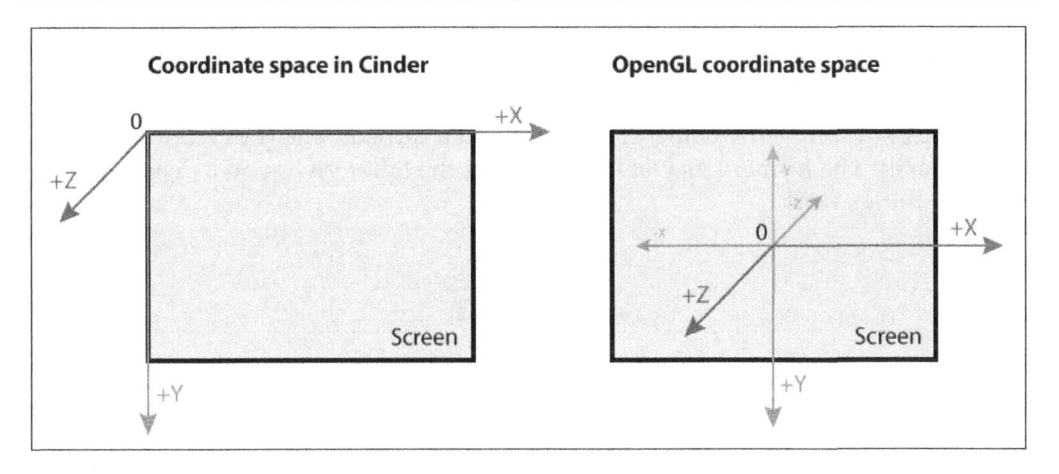

Coordinate space in Cinder | *OpenGL coordinate space*

The Cinder `gl` namespace methods does the conversion from the "top-left-centered" coordinate system to the "actually-centered" for us. So let's draw:

```
// draw a x over the whole window area
gl::drawLine( Vec2f(0.0f, 0.0f),
   Vec2f(getWindowWidth(), getWindowHeight()) );
gl::drawLine( Vec2f(0.0f, getWindowHeight()),
   Vec2f(getWindowWidth(), 0.0f) );
}
```

Compile and run the project. You should see the following output:

That's it! We've created a great base for our future applications! We are going to re-use it's structure while going through the next chapters.

Summary

In this chapter, we learned how to create a base application. We used two different approaches—a simple (by using TinderBox) and a difficult one (by creating a project from scratch). The former lets you do it fast, but the latter gives you a deeper insight into how things work.

4
Prepare Your Brushes – Drawing Basic Shapes

In this chapter, we will learn how to use Cinder for drawing different basic shapes. The shapes are basic but you can create fairly complicated images by combining these shapes. We will go through the available drawing methods one by one and try them out.

Preparing your workspace

Open TinderBox (`yourCinderPath/tools/TinderBox`) and create a new project with the name `BasicShapes`. This time enter `BasicShapes` as **Naming Prefix**. Create it somewhere safe and open up `xcode/BasicShapes.xcodeproj`. Windows users should open the project file from `vc10\BasicShapes.sln`. Open `BasicShapesApp.cpp` in the editor and navigate to a place in code that looks similar to the following snippet:

```
void BasicShapesApp::draw()
{
  // clear out the window with black
  gl::clear( Color( 0, 0, 0 ) );
}
```

This is the implementation of the main drawing method of the application. Just one line of code is executed here (`gl::clear( Color( 0, 0, 0 ) );`) and as it is already said in the comment preceding it that it clears out the color buffer with black, and it essentially means everything that has been drawn before in the previous `draw()` loop is replaced with black.

Prepare Your Brushes – Drawing Basic Shapes

The `draw()` method is being executed once per frame. The default frame rate in Cinder is 30 frames per second. So the background is cleared 30 times per second.

Let's try to change the color of the background! As you can see, you have to pass a `Color` parameter to the `gl::clear()` function. In this case the `Color` object consists of three parameters that define the color in the RGB color system. In the `Color( 0, 0, 0 )` parameter there are three zeroes inside the brackets. The first one defines the amount of red color, second is for green, and third is for blue respectively. Let's say we want the background to be red. Then, we have to pass `1` as the first parameter for the color. It should look similar to the following:

```
gl::clear( Color( 1, 0, 0 ) );
```

Compile and run the project to see if we succeeded. You should see a window with a bright-red background. Colors in Cinder are defined as numbers from 0 to 1. So if you don't want the background to be so bright, try this:

```
gl::clear( Color( 0.5f, 0, 0 ) );
```

Compile and run the project again. You should see a lesser bright-red background now. Nice! Now let's give yellow color to the background. We will need to change two of the `Color` parameters to do this as there is no separate parameter for the amount of yellow color in the RGB color system. When we look at the color wheel, we can see that yellow resides there between red and green. When we examine the space between these colors closely, you will see that, red becomes orange, orange becomes yellow, and yellow becomes green.

So we have to mix the two colors in the same amount to get the yellow color. In code it will look similar to the following:

```
gl::clear( Color( 1, 1, 0 ) );
```

Compile and run the project. Good work! You will now see a nice, bright yellow background. Let's do one last adjustment to it and change it to white. To do so, we have to set all the RGB components to their maximum values. As we know from the world of physics that white color consists of all the visible light wavelengths and when we shoot a white light beam through a glass prism, we get a rainbow – a full visible color spectrum. When we combine all the colors of the spectrum together in the same amount, we get white:

```
gl::clear( Color( 1, 1, 1 ) );
```

Now, we have a nice white background. Let's draw something on it!

Drawing lines

Let's change our background to black again and add the following lines of code:

```
// draw a line
gl::drawLine( Vec2f(0,0), Vec2f(100,100) );
```

Compile and run the project to see what happens. You should see a relatively short white line on the screen. This is what the function `gl::drawLine()` just did. As we can see, there are two parameters that have to be passed to it. The first one represents the start coordinates of the line, the second one defines the end coordinates of the line. These two points are defined as `Vec2f` objects. It is possible to tell from the name of these objects that they are vectors that store two float values. These are vectors that can be used in a two-dimensional space. `Vec2f(0,0)` represents a point in the two-dimensional space that resides at the top-left corner of the screen. Let's draw two diagonal lines across the whole window. Add the following code instead of `gl::drawLine( Vec2f(0,0), Vec2f(100,100) );`:

```
gl::drawLine( Vec2f(0,0),
Vec2f(getWindowWidth(),getWindowHeight()) );
gl::drawLine( Vec2f(0,getWindowHeight()),
Vec2f(getWindowWidth(),0) );
```

As you can see we used two new methods here, `getWindowWidth()` and `getWindowHeight()`, which are meant for determining the window size while the application is running. It is a very handy way of drawing graphics that can be independent from the window size. Instead of changing the parameters manually each time we decide to change our application window size. We can just place the `getWindowWidth()` and `getWindowHeight()` methods in place of the parameters and the graphics will be adjusted automatically whenever the application window is being resized.

Compile and run the application and try to change the size of the window by dragging its lower-right corner—the lines should adjust to the new window size.

Doing this is good but what if we need the lines to be in a color other than white? How about cyan? No problem! Add the following line of code before the `drawLine()` calls:

```
gl::color( 0, 1, 1 );
```

> **Downloading the example code**
> You can download the example code files for all Packt books you have purchased from your account at http://www.packtpub.com. If you purchased this book elsewhere, you can visit http://www.packtpub.com/support and register to have the files e-mailed directly to you.

That was not so hard. We just have to remember to change the color (if we want to) before we call a function that is supposed to draw something. So if we want to draw one line in red and another in cyan, we do it in the following way:

```
gl::color( 0, 1, 1 ); // set color to cyan
gl::drawLine( Vec2f(0,0),
Vec2f(getWindowWidth(),getWindowHeight()) );
gl::color( 1, 0, 0 ); // set color to red
gl::drawLine( Vec2f(0,getWindowHeight()),
Vec2f(getWindowWidth(),0) );
```

So now we know how to change the color of the lines. How about changing the thickness? No problem! Place the following line of code before the line draw calls:

```
glLineWidth( 10.0f );
```

So now our lines are being drawn with the thickness of 10 pixels. Compile and run the project to see how it looks. Now you should see the lines as shown in the following screenshot:

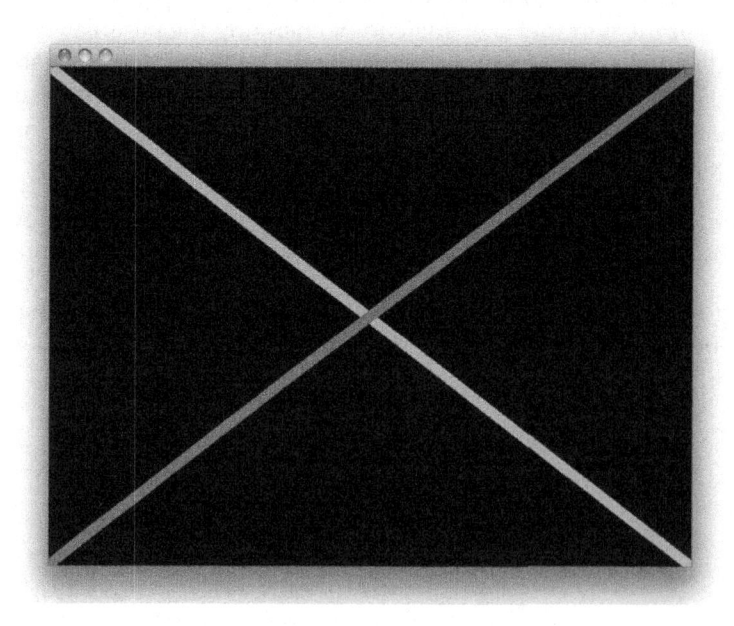

The following is the full draw method, if you failed to understand something before (I have changed the line width to 2 in the following code):

```
void BasicShapesApp::draw(){
  // clear out the window with black
  gl::clear( Color( 0, 0, 0 ) );

  // draw some lines
  glLineWidth( 2 ); // set line width to 2
  gl::color( 0, 1, 1 ); // set color to cyan
  gl::drawLine( Vec2f(0,0),
      Vec2f(getWindowWidth(),getWindowHeight()) );
  gl::color( 1, 0, 0 ); // set color to red
  gl::drawLine( Vec2f(0,getWindowHeight()),
      Vec2f(getWindowWidth(),0) );
}
```

Drawing circles

How about adding some circles to the composition? Add the following lines after the last `drawLine` call:

```
gl::drawSolidCircle( Vec2f(getWindowWidth()/2,
    getWindowHeight()/2), 50 );
```

After you compile and run the application, you should see a circle in the middle of the screen. The `drawSolidCircle()` function takes two parameters. First is the position of the center of the circle. Second is the radius of the circle. We define the position by using the `Vec2f` object again. As you can see, we use `getWindowWidth()` and `getWindowHeight()` again. This time we need them to get the center coordinates of the screen. We get it by dividing the window's width and height by 2. Again, by using these methods we make sure that our circle will be drawn in the middle of the screen no matter what size the window is.

There is a shorter way to do this though that is by using the `getWindowCenter()` method. If we use it, we get the same result but the code looks a bit more clear:

```
gl::drawSolidCircle( getWindowCenter(), 50 );
```

Let's change the color of the circle to something else. You can chose your own color, but I will use magenta this time. Add the following line of code right before the `drawSolidCircle()` function call:

```
gl::color( 1, 0, 1 ); // set color to magenta
```

Try to experiment with the position, radius, and color of the circle. Try to draw more than one shape and also try giving them different colors.

What if we want to draw just the outline of the circle? Cinder has a separate function for this called `drawStrokedCircle()`. After the `drawSolidCircle()` function add another line of code as follows:

```
gl::drawStrokedCircle( getWindowCenter(), 100 );
```

Similar to the `drawSolidCircle()` function, `drawStrokedCircle()` also takes two parameters—position and radius. The difference is just that it draws just the outline. The outline has the same thickness that we defined earlier with the help of the `glLineWidth()` function. Let's change it to something else by adding the following line of code just before the `drawStrokedCircle()` line:

```
glLineWidth( 4 );
```

Compile and run the project, and see what happens. You should see a screen similar to the following screenshot:

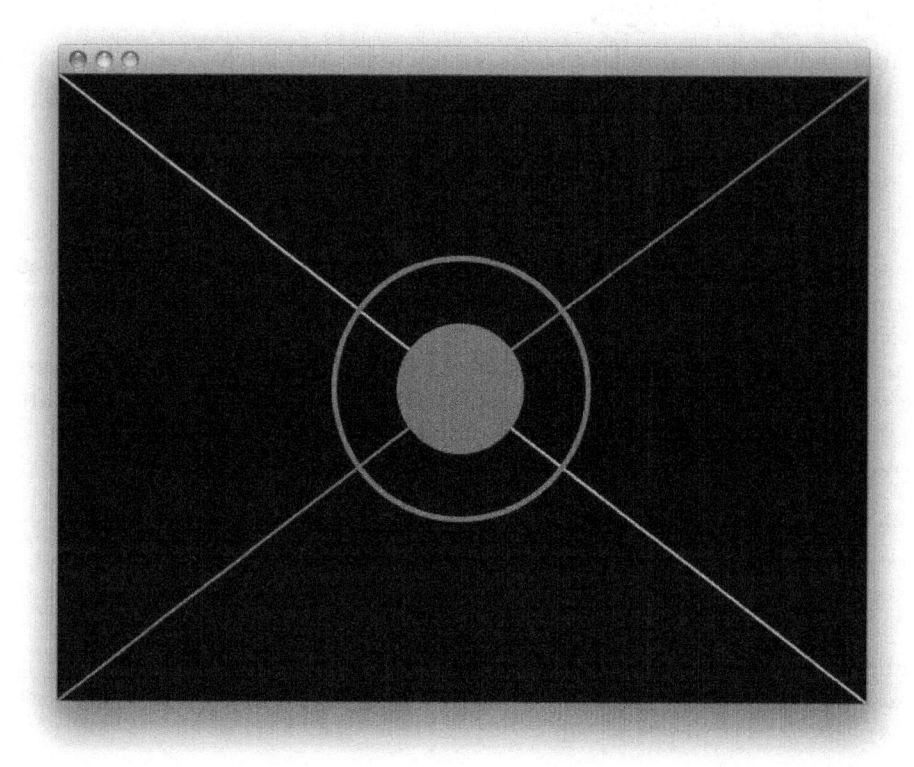

There is a hidden third parameter for the `drawSolidCircle()` and `drawStrokedCircle()` functions. As the circles are drawn by using triangles, each time a circle is being drawn, it has to be decided how many triangles to use. Cinder does it automatically but it is possible to define the triangle count by ourselves. So let's change the amount of triangle segments:

```
gl::color( 1, 0, 1 ); // set color to magenta
gl::drawSolidCircle( getWindowCenter(), 50, 5 );
glLineWidth( 4 );
gl::drawStrokedCircle( getWindowCenter(), 100, 5 );
```

Note the highlighted parts of the code. We told the circle drawing functions to draw circles by using just five triangles. By doing this we get pentagons instead of circles. Compile and run the project to see it yourself!

Try to experiment with all the properties to get the most out of it. You can draw almost any kind of regular polygon shape with this function.

Drawing rectangles

Now that we know how to draw lines and circles, let's move to another geometric primitive that we can use—the rectangle.

As in the case of a circle, there is one function for drawing a filled rectangle and one function for drawing just the outline. They are `drawSolidRect()` and `drawStrokedRect()` respectively.

```
gl::color( 0, 0, 1 ); // set color to blue
gl::drawSolidRect( Rectf( getWindowWidth()/2-20.0f,
   getWindowHeight()/2-20.0f,
   getWindowWidth()/2+20.0f,
   getWindowHeight()/2+20.0f ) );
gl::drawStrokedRect( Rectf( getWindowWidth()/2-120.0f,
   getWindowHeight()/2-120.0f,
   getWindowWidth()/2+120.0f,
   getWindowHeight()/2+120.0f ) );
```

Here we draw two rectangles, one filled (or solid) and one as an outline. Note that we pass just one parameter of the type `Rectf` to both the functions. The simplest version of `Rectf` is being constructed by using the coordinates of top-left and bottom-right corners of the rectangle. Most of the drawing APIs use x and y coordinates of the top-left corner and the width and height of the rectangle, so it could be a bit difficult to get used to this.

Prepare Your Brushes – Drawing Basic Shapes

Other useful drawing functions

These are the very basic drawing functions, and actually you can do a lot with them if you use them in a creative way. But here are a couple of other functions that are worth checking out. They are given in the following code snippet:

```
gl::color( 1, 1, 0 );
gl::drawSolidEllipse( Vec2f(150,100), 100, 50, 10);
gl::drawStrokedEllipse( Vec2f(400,300), 100, 175, 15);
gl::drawSolidRoundedRect(
Rectf(550,150,600,300), 20, 4 );
gl::drawStrokedRoundedRect(
Rectf(20,300,200,400), 10, 10 );
```

Experiment with the properties of these functions to fully understand what they mean. Compile and run the project and you should see an image similar to the following screenshot:

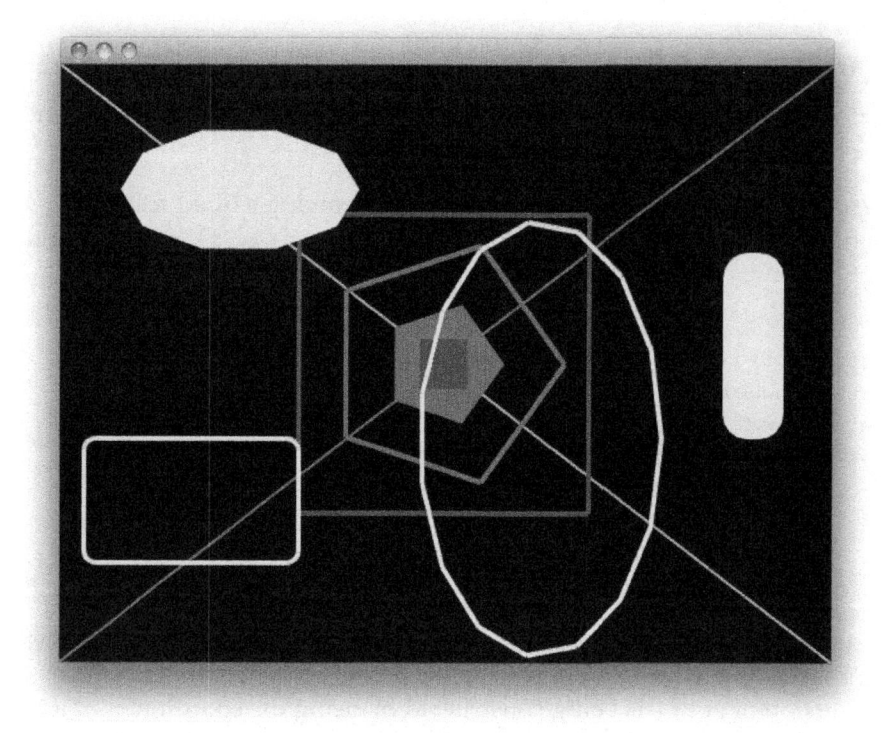

Try to re-size the window by dragging the bottom right corner. You will see the difference between graphics that are drawn relative to the window's size and the ones that are not. Keep this in mind when creating your own application.

The following is the full code for drawing all the shapes, in case you did not understand which line of code goes where:

```
void BasicShapesApp::draw(){
  // clear out the window with black
  gl::clear( Color( 0, 0, 0 ) );

  // draw some lines
  glLineWidth( 2 ); // set line width to 2
  gl::color( 0, 1, 1 ); // set color to cyan
  gl::drawLine( Vec2f(0,0),
        Vec2f(getWindowWidth(),getWindowHeight()) );
  gl::color( 1, 0, 0 ); // set color to red
  gl::drawLine( Vec2f(0,getWindowHeight()),
        Vec2f(getWindowWidth(),0) );

  // draw some circles
    gl::color( 1, 0, 1 ); // set color to magenta
    gl::drawSolidCircle( getWindowCenter(), 50, 5 );
  glLineWidth( 4 );
    gl::drawStrokedCircle( getWindowCenter(), 100, 5 );

  // draw rectangles
    gl::color( 0, 0, 1 ); // set color to blue
    gl::drawSolidRect( Rectf( getWindowWidth()/2-20.0f,
        getWindowHeight()/2-20.0f,
        getWindowWidth()/2+20.0f,
        getWindowHeight()/2+20.0f ) );
    gl::drawStrokedRect( Rectf( getWindowWidth()/2-120.0f,
        getWindowHeight()/2-120.0f,
        getWindowWidth()/2+120.0f,
        getWindowHeight()/2+120.0f ) );

  // draw rest
    gl::color( 1, 1, 0 );
    gl::drawSolidEllipse( Vec2f(150,100), 100, 50, 10);
    gl::drawStrokedEllipse( Vec2f(400,300), 100, 175, 15);
    gl::drawSolidRoundedRect(
        Rectf(550,150,600,300), 20, 4 );
    gl::drawStrokedRoundedRect(
        Rectf(20,300,200,400), 10, 10 );
}
```

That's it! This is one of the simplest way to draw basic shapes with Cinder.

Summary

In this chapter we went through the most essential drawing functions in Cinder. You can draw a lot with these. However, there are limitations of what can be done with them. If you need to draw something really complex and it has to perform well or extremely well, consider obtaining some OpenGL knowledge.

Here you can find a full list of drawing functions that are currently available in Cinder at `http://libcinder.org/docs/v0.8.4/namespacecinder_1_1gl.html`. On the web page, scroll down to the functions section and look at functions that start with "draw".

We will use some of the functions from this list in the next chapters, so this is not the only place where we use drawing.

5
Making Use of Images – Loading and Displaying

In this chapter we will learn the following:

- How to load an image
- How to display it on the screen
- About general asset handling in Cinder

You might make use of photographs, illustrations, or different image databases in your applications. To do so, you will need a way to load an image into your application and most importantly, to display it on the screen.

In this chapter we will learn the basics of Cinder file loading features and learn to load an image from the Web and local storage.

Loading an image

Open TinderBox and create a new project with the name `BasicImages`. Open `xcode/BasicImages.xcodeproj` project file. Windows users should open the project file `vc10\BasicImages.sln`. Open `BasicImagesApp.cpp` in the editor.

First we are going to include some header files that declare functionality that is required to perform the things we want to get done.

Navigate to a point in the code where there are `#include` statements and add the following lines of code just after `#include "cinder/gl/gl.h"`:

```
#include "cinder/ImageIo.h"
#include "cinder/gl/Texture.h"
```

The first include statement loads code header that is responsible for the Cinder image input/output functionality, the second code header include allows us to use OpenGL textures for drawing images on the screen.

Next we need to declare a variable of type `gl::Texture` that will contain the actual image data. You can chose your own name for that, but I will call it `imgTexture`:

```
gl::Texture imgTexture;
```

Add the highlighted line of code just after `void draw();` in the `BasicImagesApp` class declaration:

```
class BasicImagesApp : public AppBasic {
public:
  void setup();
  void update();
  void draw();
  gl::Texture imgTexture;
};
```

Next, we need to select an image to be loaded into the application. So we are going to use some random image from the internet as it is the fastest way to get a visible image on the screen if you have an internet connection.

> Before compiling and running the following example, try to open this URL http://rijnieks.lv/projects/cinder_begin_creative_coding/images/image.png in your browser. If you do not see an image, please find any other *.png or *.jpg image on the internet.

Add the following highlighted line of code in the setup method declaration:

```
void BasicImagesApp::setup() {
  imgTexture = gl::Texture( loadImage( loadUrl( Url("http://rijnieks.lv/projects/cinder_begin_creative_coding/images/image.png") ) ) );
}
```

The reason why we load it in the `setup()` is that we need to load the image just once. As loading images from the net takes some time, we don't want to delay our `draw()` or `update()` operations because the image is still loading. Cinder is about speed and we don't want to sacrifice it.

Now we need to add some code that will take care of displaying the image. Go to the implementation of the `draw()` method and add this code just after the `gl::clear( Color( 0, 0, 0 ) );` function:

```
gl::draw( imgTexture, getWindowBounds() );
```

Here we tell Cinder that we want to draw our `imgTexture` within the application window bounds (the image will be stretched so its width equals the window's width and its height equals the window's height). Try to compile and run the application. After a short delay an image should appear. If you try to resize the window, you can see that the image is being resized with it.

The member function `getWindowBounds()` returns an `Area` object and instead of using this function we can define the drawing area by ourselves. Try this:

```
gl::draw( imgTexture, Area(100,100,540,380) );
```

If you try to resize the window now, you will see that it does not affect the image as now it's display position and size is hardcoded in `Area(100,100,540,380)`.

Handling assets

Now let's see what we need to create an application that will be used on a computer without an internet connection. We have to store our image somewhere on the computer.

Cinder has a predefined way of handling images and similar assets. If you created your project with TinderBox, you may have noticed that you have an **assets** directory in your project folder. If not, create one.

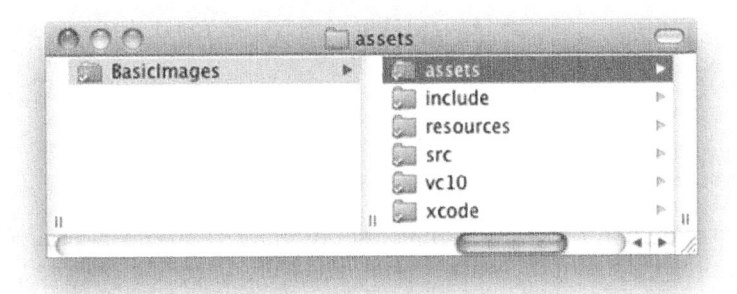

Now copy your image file into the assets directory and change the `loadImage` code in the `setup()` implementation to the following:

```
imgTexture = gl::Texture( loadImage( loadAsset( "MyImage.png" ) ) );
```

Making Use of Images – Loading and Displaying

As you can see we changed `loadUrl()` to `loadAsset()` and it actually seems simpler than the `loadUrl( Url( "http://..." ) )` approach. It's just that we do need to take care of our assets by ourselves.

Now try to move the assets directory one level up in the filesystem so it is next to the `BasicImages` folder as shown in the following screenshot:

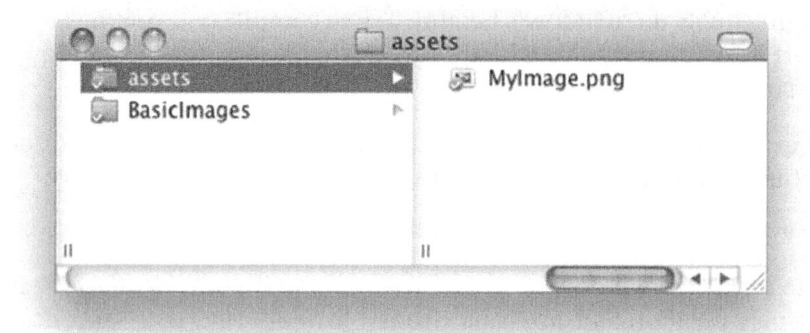

Try to compile and run our project and you will be surprised that the image still loads! Some people may think that this is the magic of caching or something similar but no, Cinder just automatically searches for the `assets` directory up to five levels above the executable. So you can choose at what level you want to store your assets, but in a way the default way may be the best as it allows you to use the same assets for your Mac OS X and Windows projects. If you are working on more than one project with the same assets, then you may move your `assets` directory to the projects folder level as we just did.

There is one small detail to it—if your image uses alpha transparency, you might get strange results. To draw images with alpha transparency, we have to enable alpha blending before drawing the image and disable it after it is drawn by adding the following code snippet:

```
gl::enableAlphaBlending();
gl::draw( imgTexture, Rectf(100,100,540,380) );
gl::disableAlphaBlending();
```

There is also a way of adding additional asset directories in case you have more than one group of projects using the same assets. The following line of code takes care of that:

```
addAssetDirectory( "/Users/You/myOtherAssets/" );
```

Note that you have to use an absolute path here, so this is not too good for cross-platform projects. In windows you might write something similar to the following:

```
addAssetDirectory( "C:\Users\You\myOtherAssets\" );
```

If you use assets, you have to remember to deploy the assets directory with your application.

There is a way that tells you how to include assets inside the application, but this topic is a bit outside the scope of this book. You should search the Internet for "Cinder resource management" if you want to know more about it.

The following is the full code of the application that we made in this chapter:

```
#include "cinder/app/AppBasic.h"
#include "cinder/gl/gl.h"
#include "cinder/ImageIo.h"
#include "cinder/gl/Texture.h"

using namespace ci;
using namespace ci::app;
using namespace std;

class BasicImagesApp : public AppBasic {
public:
  void setup();
  void draw();
  gl::Texture imgTexture;
};

void BasicImagesApp::setup() {
  addAssetDirectory( "/Users/kr15h/myOtherAssets/" );
  imgTexture = gl::Texture( loadImage( loadAsset( "MyImage.png" ) ) );
}

void BasicImagesApp::draw() {
  gl::clear( Color( 0, 0, 0 ) );
  gl::enableAlphaBlending();
  gl::draw( imgTexture, Rectf(100,100,540,380) );
  gl::disableAlphaBlending();
}


CINDER_APP_BASIC( BasicImagesApp, RendererGl )
```

Not a lot of code!

Summary

In this chapter we learned how to load an image from the Internet as well as from local storage, assign it to an OpenGL texture, and draw it on the screen.

We gained a basic understanding on how asset management works in Cinder and that we don't have to worry about the location of the assets directory as long as it is less than five levels up from our application.

We also understood that we can use the loadUrl() and loadAsset() functions in the same way on Mac OS X and Windows.

6
Accelerate – Creating Generative Animation

In this chapter we are going to learn the following:

- Basics of procedural animation
- Animating multiple objects at the same time
- How to make use of randomness
- How to benefit from built-in animation easing functions

We will create a relatively simple drawing by using basic shapes and then animate these shapes in a parametric way. We will also learn how to make use of built-in easing functions of Cinder that can make polishing our animations a lot easier.

Preparing the stage

Before we begin, open TinderBox and create a new project with the name `BasicAnimation`. Open `xcode/BasicAnimation.xcodeproj` (`vc10\BasicAnimation.sln` on Windows). Open `BasicAnimationApp.cpp` in the editor so that we can start making changes.

Accelerate – Creating Generative Animation

We are going to change the window size this time as 640 x 480 px might be too small for most of the compositions we will want to create later. To do that, we need to override another Cinder `AppBasic` method—`prepareSettings()`. Add a new declaration just after the `draw()` method declaration as follows:

```
class BasicAnimationApp : public AppBasic {
public:
  void setup();
  void update();
  void draw();
  void prepareSettings( Settings *settings );
};
```

Now add the implementation of the method that we just declared just before the implementation of the `setup()` method:

```
void BasicAnimationApp::prepareSettings( Settings *settings ){}
```

Let's change the window size. To do that, add the following line of code inside the `prepareSettings` method implementation:

```
settings->setWindowSize( 800, 600 );
```

We will also change the frame rate to something more appropriate for Cinder—60 frames per second is a good choice:

```
settings->setFrameRate( 60 );
```

So, this altogether looks as follows:

```
void BasicAnimationApp::prepareSettings( Settings *settings ){
  settings->setWindowSize( 800, 600 );
  settings->setFrameRate( 60 );
}
```

Now compile and run your application to test if it works.

Next we are going to draw a solid circle. As you might remember from the previous chapters, we have to use the `drawSolidCircle()` function in order to do that.

Navigate to the `draw()` member function implementation in the `BasicAnimationApp.cpp` file and add the following line of code just after the `gl::clear()` function call:

```
gl::drawSolidCircle( getWindowCenter(), 30 );
```

This draws a white circle with a radius of 30 pixels in the center of the window. As this chapter is about animation, let's think of some ways to move this circle.

Adding animation

As we already know, in each frame before we draw something, we use black color to clear everything that is left there from the previous frame. We use `gl::clear()` to do that. To create the effect of moving something, we need to change the object's position in each frame.

To do that, we will need to replace the values of the `drawSolidCircle` position parameters to variables. Let's declare a new variable that will hold the position of the circle on the screen:

```
    void prepareSettings( Settings *settings );
    Vec2f currentPosition;
};
```

This variable will hold the x and y position of the circle that we are drawing inside the `draw()` method.

Now we will set the initial value of the variable in the `setup()` method:

```
void BasicAnimationApp::setup() {
  currentPosition = getWindowCenter();
}
```

Accelerate – Creating Generative Animation

As you can see, a part of the preceding code snippet is the same as we used in the `drawSolidCircle()` function call. We just made it changeable.

Finally, we have to replace the values in the `drawSolidCircle()` function to the newly created variable:

```
void BasicAnimationApp::draw() {
  gl::clear( Color( 0, 0, 0 ) );
  gl::drawSolidCircle( currentPosition, 30 );
}
```

Compile and run our application. Nothing much has changed. Don't worry about that and add the following line of code before the `drawSolidCircle()` function call:

```
currentPosition.x++;
```

Compile and run the application again and there it is, a moving circle. Cool! We have our first animation! Now let's do something with the radius of the circle. To apply animation to it, we have to declare a new variable again:

```
void prepareSettings( Settings *settings );
Vec2f currentPosition;
float circleRadius;
};
```

Now, set its starting value:

```
void BasicAnimationApp::setup() {
  currentPosition = getWindowCenter();
  circleRadius = 100;
}
```

And add an animation rule and replace the constant value of the circle radius parameter of the `drawSolidCircle()` function call in the `draw()` method implementation:

```
currentPosition.x++;
circleRadius--;
gl::drawSolidCircle( currentPosition, circleRadius );
}
```

Compile and run our application. You should see a big white point disappearing in front of your eyes. It might seem that you did something wrong, but don't worry, everything is correct. The trick is that we decreased the circle radius by one pixel for each frame. It is happening at a rate of 60 times per second and that means that the radius of the circle will reach 0 in approximately 1.5 seconds. Therefore, if the radius is 0, the circle becomes invisible as there can be no circle without a radius.

So far so good. Let's try to move our circle to some fixed location over time. Let's say we want to move it from the top-left corner of the screen to the bottom right. To do that we need to set the initial position of the circle to 0. and let's change the initial `circleRadius` to something smaller as well:

```
void BasicAnimationApp::setup() {
  currentPosition = Vec2f(0,0);
  circleRadius = 100;
}
```

Let's declare another `Vec2f` variable that will hold the target position of the circle in the class declaration:

```
Vec2f currentPosition;
Vec2f targetPosition;
float circleRadius;
};
```

We need to set the initial target position somewhere, so we have to add a new line in the `setup()` method implementation:

```
void BasicAnimationApp::setup() {
  currentPosition = Vec2f(0,0);
  targetPosition = Vec2f(800,600);
  circleRadius = 100;
}
```

Finally, we need to write some code that creates a smooth transition between `currentPosition` and `targetPosition`. Let's do it in the `update()` method implementation as it is meant for such calculations. Remember, try to use the `draw()` method just for drawing and place all your calculations inside `update()`. It does not matter much for a small application such as this one, but as your code grows bigger, it is possible that the application won't perform so well or will even crash if you don't stick to this simple rule.

```
void BasicAnimationApp::update() {
  Vec2f difference = targetPosition - currentPosition;
  difference *= 0.95f;
  currentPosition = targetPosition - difference;
}
```

These three lines of code calculate the difference between the current circle position and the target circle position. Then, we make the difference between these positions smaller by multiplying it with a floating point number that is smaller than 0. Finally, we calculate the new current position by subtracting the new difference from the target position of the circle.

Accelerate – Creating Generative Animation

This would require a longer code if we didn't make use of the integrated vector algebra features of Cinder. As a `Vec2f` object contains two values (the x and the y coordinate), when we multiply it with a single value, both values inside the `Vec2f` object are multiplied by this value. Furthermore, if we multiply a `Vec2f` object with another `Vec2f` object, the first element of the first vector is multiplied with the first element of the second one, and the second element of the first one is multiplied with the second element of the second one, and so on.

Now compile and run our application. You should see a circle moving from the top-left corner to the bottom-right corner of the screen.

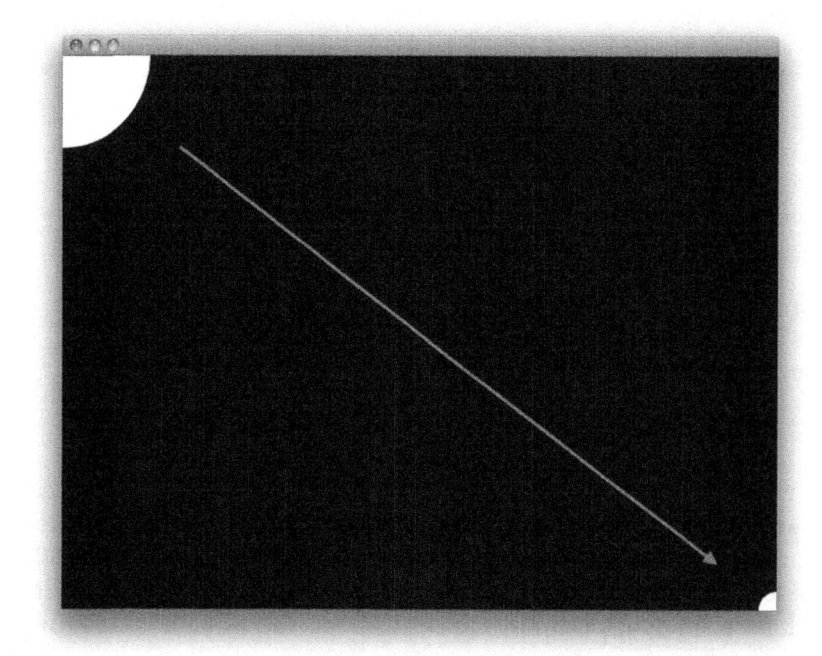

Adding randomness

Let's add a bit of unpredictability to this by using the almighty random functions. To use them in Cinder, you have to include a header file that contains the necessary code:

```
#include "cinder/Rand.h"
```

[66]

Add this in the beginning of the `BasicAnimationApp.cpp` file. Next, we need to calculate random target position in the `setup()` method implementation:

```
void BasicAnimationApp::setup() {
  currentPosition = Vec2f(0,0);
  targetPosition.x = Rand::randFloat(0, getWindowWidth());
  targetPosition.y = Rand::randFloat(0, getWindowHeight());
  circleRadius = 100;
}
```

Now each time you run the application, a different end position will be calculated and the circle will fly to a different place on the screen.

Let's change the current position of the circle to something random as well:

```
void BasicAnimationApp::setup() {
  currentPosition.x = Rand::randFloat(0, getWindowWidth());
  currentPosition.y = Rand::randFloat(0, getWindowHeight());
  targetPosition.x = Rand::randFloat(0, getWindowWidth());
  targetPosition.y = Rand::randFloat(0, getWindowHeight());
  circleRadius = 100;
}
```

Compile and run the application to see the change.

It might seem a bit boring to see just one random animation after you have opened an application. People usually expect something more. So how about we calculate a new random end position as the circle reaches its current end position? Ok, let's do that! Add the following piece of code in the `update()` method implementation just after `currentPosition = targetPosition - difference;`:

```
if ( currentPosition.distance(targetPosition) < 1.0f ) {
  targetPosition.x = Rand::randFloat(0, getWindowWidth());
  targetPosition.y = Rand::randFloat(0, getWindowHeight());
}
```

Comment out or delete the following highlighted lines from the `draw()` method:

```
gl::clear( Color( 0, 0, 0 ) );
//currentPosition.x++;
//circleRadius--;
gl::drawSolidCircle( currentPosition, circleRadius );
```

Compile and run our application. This is a bit more interesting, but still it needs something more to be complete.

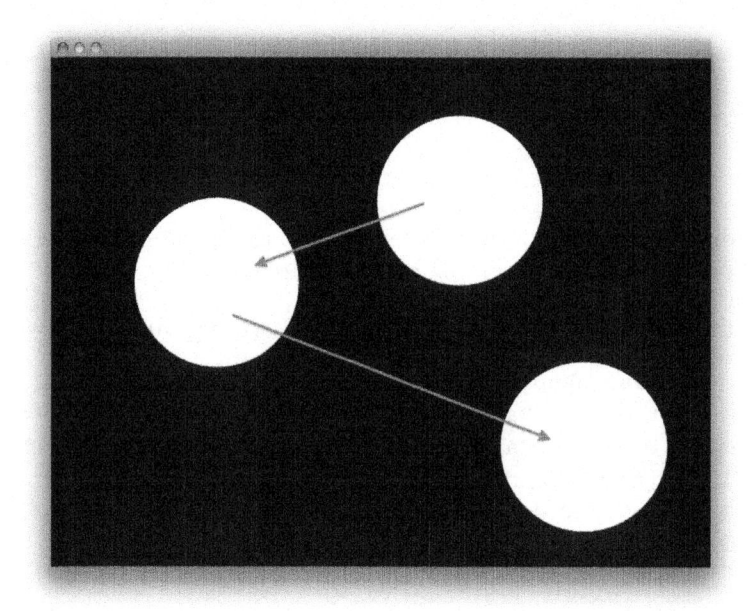

How about we try to handle more than one circle on the screen? It would be worth explaining how to create a particle system as a separate class, but this won't fit in the scope of this book, so we will continue to make some changes in the same file.

More circles

Let's define the count of the circles that we want the application to handle. Add the following line of code just after the `#include` statements:

```
#define CIRCLE_COUNT 100
```

Now, let's go to the class declaration part and change the declarations of our variables to arrays:

```
Vec2f currentPosition[CIRCLE_COUNT];
Vec2f targetPosition[CIRCLE_COUNT];
float circleRadius[CIRCLE_COUNT];
```

As you can see, we used the previously defined constant as the size of our arrays. By doing that we can change the circle count easily later.

Next, we have to change some code in the `setup()` method implementation:

```
void BasicAnimationApp::setup() {
  for(int i=0; i<CIRCLE_COUNT; i++) {
    currentPosition[i].x=Rand::randFloat(0,getWindowWidth());
    currentPosition[i].y=Rand::randFloat(0,getWindowHeight());
    targetPosition[i].x=Rand::randFloat(0,getWindowWidth());
    targetPosition[i].y=Rand::randFloat(0,getWindowHeight());
    circleRadius[i] = Rand::randFloat(1, 10);
  }
}
```

Basically, we wrapped the same code we had before into a `for` loop that iterates over all our parameter arrays and sets initial values for each of them.

Don't compile yet as we still have to make changes to the `update()` and `draw()` methods in a similar way. Change our `update()` method as follows:

```
void BasicAnimationApp::update() {
  Vec2f difference;
  for (int i=0; i<CIRCLE_COUNT; i++) {
    difference = targetPosition[i] - currentPosition[i];
    difference *= 0.95f;
    currentPosition[i] = targetPosition[i] - difference;

    if (currentPosition[i].distance(targetPosition[i]) < 1.0f) {
      targetPosition[i].x =
      Rand::randFloat(0,getWindowWidth());
      targetPosition[i].y =
      Rand::randFloat(0,getWindowHeight());
    }
  }
}
```

And lastly, change our `draw()` method implementation as follows:

```
void BasicAnimationApp::draw() {
  gl::clear( Color( 0, 0, 0 ) );
  for (int i=0; i<CIRCLE_COUNT; i++) {
    gl::drawSolidCircle( currentPosition[i], circleRadius[i] );
  }
}
```

Accelerate – Creating Generative Animation

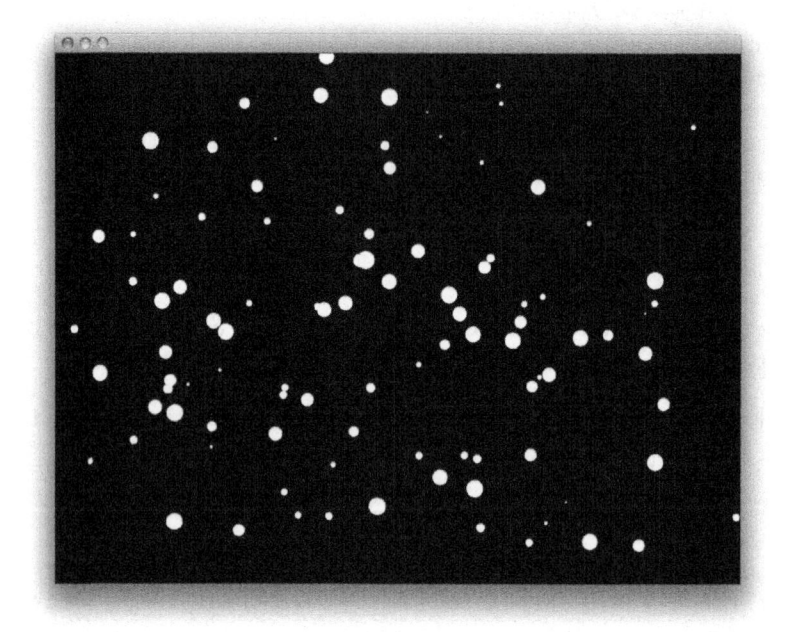

Compile and run our application now. This looks a bit more interesting!

It seems that 100 circles are not enough, so how about we set the `CIRCLE_COUNT` constant to `1000`?

```
#define CIRCLE_COUNT 1000
```

No problem!

But what if we don't want to focus on quantity, but on the quality of movement? This is where animation easing joins the game.

Using built-in eases

Now, say we want to make use of the easing algorithms that we saw in the `EaseGallery` sample. To do that, we have to change the code by following certain steps.

To use the easing functions, we have to include the `Easing.h` header file:

```
#include "cinder/Easing.h"
```

First we are going to add two more variables, `startPostition` and `circleTimeBase`:

```
Vec2f startPosition[CIRCLE_COUNT];
Vec2f currentPosition[CIRCLE_COUNT];
Vec2f targetPosition[CIRCLE_COUNT];
float circleRadius[CIRCLE_COUNT];
float circleTimeBase[CIRCLE_COUNT];
```

Then, in the `setup()` method implementation, we have to change the `currentPosition` parts to `startPosition` and add an initial value to the `circleTimeBase` array members:

```
startPosition[i].x = Rand::randFloat(0, getWindowWidth());
startPosition[i].y = Rand::randFloat(0, getWindowHeight());
circleTimeBase[i] = 0;
```

Next, we have to change the `update()` method so that it can be used along with the easing functions. They are based on time and they return a floating point value between 0 and 1 that defines the `playhead` position on an abstract 0 to 1 timeline:

```
void BasicAnimationApp::update() {
  Vec2f difference;
  for (int i=0; i<CIRCLE_COUNT; i++) {
    difference = targetPosition[i] - startPosition[i];
    currentPosition[i] = easeOutExpo(
      getElapsedSeconds()-circleTimeBase[i]) *
      difference + startPosition[i];

    if ( currentPosition[i].distance(targetPosition[i])
    < 1.0f )
    {
      targetPosition[i].x =
      Rand::randFloat(0, getWindowWidth());
      targetPosition[i].y =
      Rand::randFloat(0, getWindowHeight());
      startPosition[i] = currentPosition[i];
      circleTimeBase[i] = getElapsedSeconds();
    }
  }
}
```

The highlighted parts in the preceding code snippet are those that have been changed. The most important part of it is the currentPosition[i] calculation part. We take the distance between the start and end points of the timeline and multiply it with the position floating point number that is being returned by our easing function, which in this case is easeOutExpo(). Again, it returns a floating point variable between 0 and 1 that represents the position on an abstract 0 to 1 timeline. If we multiply any number with, say, 0.33f, we get one-third of that number, 0.5f, we get one-half of that number, and so on. So, we add this distance to the circle's starting position and we get it's current position!

Compile and run our application now. You should see something as follows:

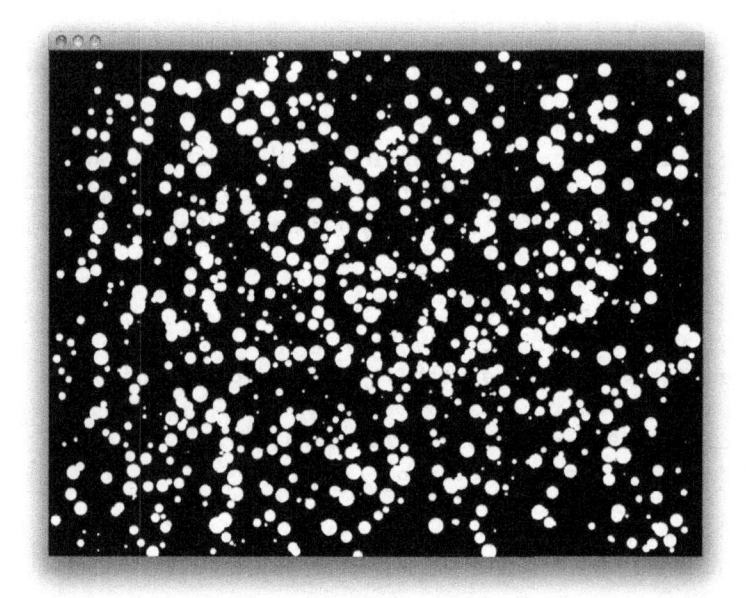

Almost like a snow storm! We will add a small modification to the code though. I will add a TWEEN_SPEED definition at the top of the code and multiply the time parameter passed to the ease function with it, so we can control the speed of the circles:

```
#define TWEEN_SPEED 0.2
```

Change the following line in the update() method implementation:

```
currentPosition[i] = easeOutExpo(
  (getElapsedSeconds()-circleTimeBase[i])*TWEEN_SPEED) *
  difference + startPosition[i];
```

I did this because the default time base for each tween is 1 second. That means that each transition is happening exactly for 1 second and that's a bit too fast for our current situation. We want it to be slower, so we multiply the time we pass to the easing function with a floating point number that is less than `1.0f` and greater than `0.0f`. By doing that we ensure that the time is scaled down and instead of 1 second we get 5 seconds for our transition.

So try to compile and run this, and see for yourself! Here is the full source code of our circle-creation:

```cpp
#include "cinder/app/AppBasic.h"
#include "cinder/gl/gl.h"
#include "cinder/Rand.h"
#include "cinder/Easing.h"

#define CIRCLE_COUNT 100
#define TWEEN_SPEED 0.2

using namespace ci;
using namespace ci::app;
using namespace std;

class BasicAnimationApp : public AppBasic {
  public:
    void setup();
    void update();
    void draw();

    void prepareSettings( Settings *settings );
    Vec2f startPosition[CIRCLE_COUNT];
    Vec2f currentPosition[CIRCLE_COUNT];
    Vec2f targetPosition[CIRCLE_COUNT];
    float circleRadius[CIRCLE_COUNT];
    float circleTimeBase[CIRCLE_COUNT];
};

void BasicAnimationApp::prepareSettings( Settings *settings ) {
    settings->setWindowSize(800,600);
    settings->setFrameRate(60);
}
```

```cpp
void BasicAnimationApp::setup() {
  for(int i=0; i<CIRCLE_COUNT; i++) {
    currentPosition[i].x=Rand::randFloat(0, getWindowWidth());
    currentPosition[i].y=Rand::randFloat(0, getWindowHeight());
    targetPosition[i].x=Rand::randFloat(0, getWindowWidth());
    targetPosition[i].y=Rand::randFloat(0, getWindowHeight());
    circleRadius[i] = Rand::randFloat(1, 10);
    startPosition[i].x = Rand::randFloat(0, getWindowWidth());
    startPosition[i].y = Rand::randFloat(0, getWindowHeight());
    circleTimeBase[i] = 0;
  }
}

void BasicAnimationApp::update() {
  Vec2f difference;
  for (int i=0; i<CIRCLE_COUNT; i++) {
    difference = targetPosition[i] - startPosition[i];
    currentPosition[i] = easeOutExpo(
      (getElapsedSeconds()-circleTimeBase[i]) *
      TWEEN_SPEED) *
      difference + startPosition[i];

      if ( currentPosition[i].distance(
      targetPosition[i]) < 1.0f )
    {
      targetPosition[i].x =
      Rand::randFloat(0, getWindowWidth());
      targetPosition[i].y =
      Rand::randFloat(0, getWindowHeight());
      startPosition[i] = currentPosition[i];
      circleTimeBase[i] = getElapsedSeconds();
    }
  }
}

void BasicAnimationApp::draw() {
  gl::clear( Color( 0, 0, 0 ) );
  for (int i=0; i<CIRCLE_COUNT; i++) {
    gl::drawSolidCircle( currentPosition[i], circleRadius[i] );
  }
}

CINDER_APP_BASIC( BasicAnimationApp, RendererGl )
```

Experiment with the properties and try to change the eases. Not all of them will work with this example, but at least you will understand how to use them to create smooth animations with Cinder.

Summary

In this chapter, we created our first generative animation application. We learned how to use instance variables for creating smooth movements and random functions to generate unpredictable results in predictable scale. We also used static arrays to change the count of the circles in the simulation and made use of Cinder easing functions that can prove themselves very handy when creating Flash-like applications (you might know the TweenLite tweening library, if you have some Flash coding background).

Finally, we tested the application with a relatively high amount of objects. This part should prove to you the real power of Cinder as you might know that creating a similar application with other frameworks based on non-C++ platforms does not run as smooth as this one.

In the next chapter, we will talk about real-time post-processing and basic methods for applying image, as well as video effects with Cinder.

7
Working with Images – Real-time Postprocessing and Effects

In this chapter we will talk about basic approaches of using built-in Cinder classes for applying effects to still and moving images.

In this chapter we will learn the following:

- Understanding the difference between CPU and GPU image processing
- Applying basic effects to images
- Looping through pixels of an image as well as a movie frame
- Making use of the pixel-level access

Introducing Texture, Surface, and Channel

In *Chapter 5, Making Use of Images – Loading and Displaying,* we already learned how to load an image into Cinder. The following is the essence of the code we used there:

```
gl::Texture texture = loadImage( loadAsset( "image.jpg" ) );
```

With this line of code we load pixels from the `image.jpg` image file into the GPU memory. `Texture` is meant for storing the image data but not for manipulating or displaying it. To show the image on the screen, we use the following line of code:

```
gl::draw( texture );
```

Say we want to do some image processing in between the load and draw stages. To process images on the GPU (where the image data is stored by the `Texture` objects), we would use shaders. Shaders make use of the OpenGL Shading Language and we won't go in detail about this now as it is way outside the scope of this book.

There is another way of processing the image, that is by loading the image on the CPU. To make use of the CPU, we have to use the `Surface` class. It is similar to the `Texture` class but the main difference is that it stores the image data on the CPU. By loading an image on the CPU, we can do the image processing with the C++ code.

To draw a surface, we will need to convert it to a `Texture` instance. It is possible to convert the `Surface` data to the `Texture` class instances for drawing something similar to the following:

```
Surface surface;
gl::Texture texture = gl::Texture( surface );
```

By performing the preceding code, we create a GPU friendly texture for displaying it on the screen.

There is a third image datatype in Cinder, the `Channel` class. If the `Surface` class is able to hold red, green, blue, and alpha values in separate channels within one object, then `Channel` makes use of just one channel (can hold one of the channels mentioned) and can be used to store grayscale images.

It is possible to create a `Surface` instance from a `Channel` class by adding the following line:

```
Surface surface( channel );
```

The preceding line of code makes it is possible to create a high-quality, grayscale image as a `Channel` class instance by passing a `Surface` instance to the `Channel` directly.

```
Channel channel( surface );
```

Applying the grayscale effect

In the previous section, we already discussed one of the basic effects that can be applied in almost every image processing software out there, grayscale. Let's create a simple application that loads an image and converts it to grayscale by using methods we just discussed.

Open up **TinderBox** and make a new application with the name `BasicEffects`. Place an image (let's call it `OurImage.png`, I will be using a simple, digitally enhanced hand-drawn sketch from my own archives) in the assets directory of the project and open the `xcode/BasicEffects.xcodeproj` project file. Windows users can open the `vc10\BasicEffects.sln` file.

Open `BasicEfectsApp.cpp` in your editor and include a couple of headers that we will need later:

```
#include "cinder/ImageIo.h"
#include "cinder/gl/Texture.h"
#include "cinder/Surface.h"
```

Now declare the variables/objects of type `Texture` and `Surface` as follows:

```
Surface surface;
gl::Texture texture;
```

Also, load an image into the `surface` object and pass it to the `Texture` constructor so we can draw it afterwards (this goes in to the `setup()` method implementation):

```
surface = Surface( loadImage( loadAsset("OurImage.png") ) );
texture = gl::Texture(surface);
```

Finally go to the `draw()` method implementation and add the following lines of code to draw the texture:

```
if ( texture ) gl::draw( texture );
```

Before we draw the texture, we need to make sure that it actually exists.

When you compile and run the project our image should appear on the screen. If it does not, make sure that the image really exists in our project's `assets` directory and that the image filename argument in the `loadAsset("OurImage.png")` is correct.

We have made the very basic structure for image processing on the CPU. To make the image in grayscale, we will make use of the `Channel` class. First, we will include the `Channel.h` file as follows:

```
#include "cinder/Channel.h"
```

Next, in the `setup()` method implementation, where we load the image, create a `Channel` instance from the `Surface` instance and construct the texture by using the newly created channel:

```
surface = Surface( loadImage( loadAsset("image.png") ) );
Channel channel( surface );
texture = gl::Texture( channel );
```

Compile and run the project. The following screenshot is a comparison image that shows the difference between the result when we use the `Surface` object for constructing a texture and `Channel`:

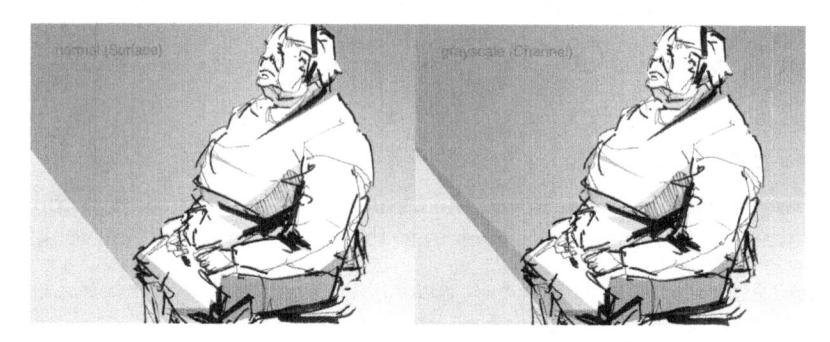

The image is automatically converted to grayscale once we pass it to the `Channel` constructor and we use the result for creating the texture. You should see it yourself when you compile and run the program.

Using threshold

Now we are going to use some per-pixel manipulation. We will choose one certain threshold value between 0 and 255 and compare each channel of each pixel to that value. If the value is above the threshold, we will change the channel value to maximum (255). If the value is less, we will change it to the minimum (0).

> Previously we were using floating point numbers from 0 to 1 to describe R, G, and B channels. When using `Surface` objects and images in general, you might want to know that each pixel of each channel of the `Surface` (`Surface8u`) object consists of 8 bits that can hold 256 values from 0 to 255 if not defined otherwise.

As we are dealing with a still image, we have to do this process only once, in the `setup()` method between the `surface` and `texture` object initialization. We will make use of a really handy helper class, `Surface::Iter`, that will allow us to loop seamlessly through lines (rows) and individual pixels of each line.

So this is the code that we have to add to the `setup()` method implementation between the `surface` and `texture` variable initialization lines as follows:

```
surface = Surface( loadImage( loadAsset("OurImage.png") ) );

int threshold = 200;
Area area = surface.getBounds();
Surface::Iter iter = surface.getIter( area );
while( iter.line() ) {
  while( iter.pixel() ) {
    iter.r() = iter.r() > threshold ? 255 : 0;
    iter.g() = iter.g() > threshold ? 255 : 0;
    iter.b() = iter.b() > threshold ? 255 : 0;
  }
}

texture = gl::Texture( surface );
```

First we define the threshold, all the values above that will be changed to 255 and all the values below or equal will be changed to 0. Say goodbye to smooth gradients. Next we get the area of the image that we will change. To change the whole image, we have to get the bounds of the whole surface. We have to get an iterator (`iter`) to construct a nice nested loop afterwards. Finally we use the iterator to loop through all the lines (rows) and pixels (columns inside the row) of the surface and change it's pixels one by one.

Don't forget to change the `Texture` initialization (you have to use our `Surface` instance again instead of `Channel`):

```
texture = gl::Texture( **surface** );
```

Note that we initialize the texture after we make changes to the pixels of the surface. Every time you make changes to the `Surface` object that you will be using as a `Texture` afterwards, you have to reinitialize the `texture` variable from the changed `Surface` object.

Compile and run the project, and see what happens! The following screenshot shows the comparison between the source image and the one with our threshold filter applied:

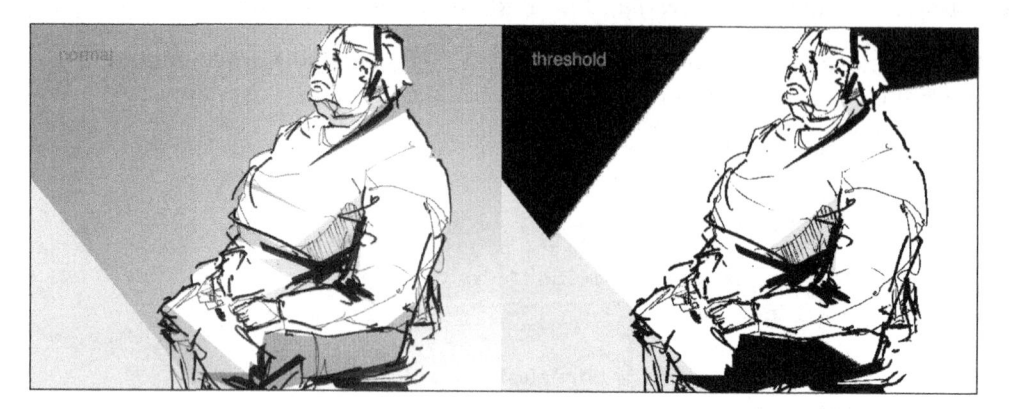

Try to experiment a bit by changing the threshold value and the way pixel values are being changed before we move on to the next part.

Animating effects

Let's make a simple effect animation by using the tricks we just learned and the `update()` method. We have to modify the code in the `setup()` method implementation so it looks similar to the following:

```
surface = Surface( loadImage( loadAsset("OurImage.png") ) );

// int threshold = 200; // comment or remove this line
Area area = surface.getBounds();
Surface::Iter iter = surface.getIter( area );
while( iter.line() ) {
  while( iter.pixel() ) {
    iter.r() += 1;
    iter.g() += 2;
    iter.b() += 3;
  }
}

texture = gl::Texture( surface );
```

Next we have to cut and paste all the code except the `surface` initialization to the `update()` method implementation as follows:

```
void BasicEffectsApp::setup() {
  surface = Surface( loadImage( loadAsset("OurImage.png") ) );
}

void BasicEffectsApp::update() {
  Area area = surface.getBounds();
  Surface::Iter iter = surface.getIter( area );
  while( iter.line() ) {
    while( iter.pixel() ) {
      iter.r() += 1;
      iter.g() += 2;
      iter.b() += 3;
    }
  }

  texture = gl::Texture( surface );
}
```

With that done, compile and run the project, and see what happens:

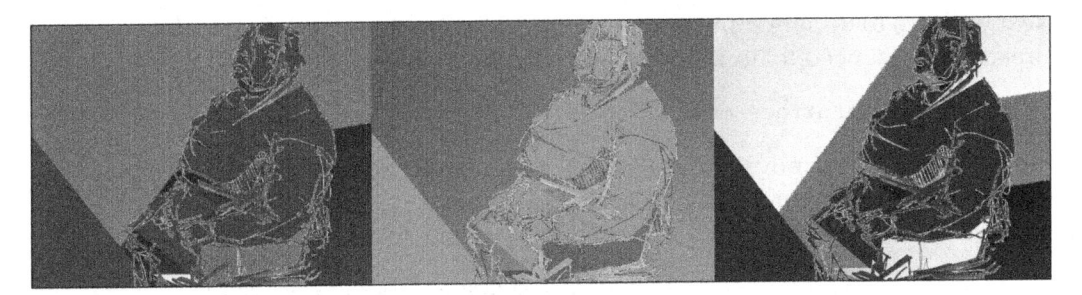

In the preceding screenshot you can see an animation that looks like some kind of acid eating and that transforms all the surfaces of the image.

Applying effects to moving images

We just saw how to get moving effects, let's try to add effects to a moving image.

Before we do that, it is a good idea to make a copy of our project (`BasicEffects`). Let's rename the folder of the new project to `BasicEffectsMotion`. Open the project file (`xcode/BasicEffects.xcodeproj` on Ma OS X or `vc10\BasicEffects.sln` on Windows).

Working with Images – Real-time Postprocessing and Effects

> For Windows users, you will have to add `QTMLClient.lib` and `CVClient.lib` to **Linker | Input | Additional Dependencies** in the project properties. You will also have to add path to the QuickTime SDK (`C:\QuickTimeSDK-7.3\Libraries`) in **Linker | General | Additional Library Directories** in the project properties. You can access project properties from the menu bar by clicking on **Project | BasicEffects Properties**.

First we need to find a movie file that we can use. `http://vimeo.com/groups/freehd` seems a good place where you can find free video footage. I found one with a footage of an industrial site.

Place the movie file in the `assets` folder of the project, open the code editor, and start with including the `QuickTime.h` file:

```
#include "cinder/qtime/QuickTime.h"
```

> In case you are using the AppRewrite version of Cinder, you should know that QuickTime has been made as a separate block. Blocks are extensions of Cinder that you can add to your project when you need a specific extra functionality.

Next we have to declare some new variables. Since we have a surface and a texture already, we just need to declare a variable for the movie:

```
qtime::MovieSurface movie;
```

With that done, let's move to the `setup()` method part and load the movie by adding the following highlighted code:

```
// comment out or remove this line
// surface = Surface( loadImage( loadAsset("OurImage.png") ) );

// add these lines
movie = qtime::MovieSurface( getAssetPath("OurMovie.mp4") );
movie.setLoop();
movie.play();
```

Next we have to copy each frame to a surface and transform that surface to a texture so we can draw it on the screen. Let's move to the `update()` method implementation to do that, remove all the previous code and add the following:

```
if ( movie.checkNewFrame() ) {
  surface = movie.getSurface();
  // add effects here
  if ( surface ) texture = gl::Texture( surface );
}
```

As loading the movie is an asynchronous process, we have to check if there is a surface before we pass it to the texture. In the same way we have to check if we have a texture before we draw it. Change the `gl::draw` part in the `draw()` method to the following:

```
if ( texture ) gl::draw( texture, getWindowBounds() );
```

We need to make sure that the movie is being drawn within the bounds of our application window. We make sure of that by passing the result of the `getWindowBounds()` function as the second parameter to the `gl::draw()` function.

Compile and run the project now. You should see the movie playing. Now we are going to combine this with the effect we made earlier. Find the place in the `update()` method between the `surface` and `texture` initialization (I left a comment `// add effects here` there). Add the following code there:

```
if ( surface ) {
  Area area = surface.getBounds();
  Surface::Iter iter = surface.getIter( area );
  while( iter.line() ) {
    while( iter.pixel() ) {
      iter.r() += addR;
      iter.g() += addG;
      iter.b() += addB;
    }
  }
  addR += 1;
  addG += 2;
  addB += 3;
}
```

As you probably must have already guessed, now we have to declare the `addR`, `addG`, and `addB` variables and set their initial values as follows:

```
// add this in the class declaration
uint8_t addR, addG, addB;

// add this in the setup() implementation
addR = addG = addB = 0;
```

Compile and run the project. You should see the colors of the movie changing as shown in the following screenshot:

Experiment with the `addR`, `addG`, and `addB` values to see what kind of different effects you are able to get out of this.

Summary

In this chapter, we learned the basic methods of applying effects to still and moving images. It is possible to do a lot more by studying the raw image processing algorithms and applying them as per-pixel operations. So if you do that and you are able to reproduce most of the image effects that one can find in Photoshop or Gimp—congratulations! You may also want to bring your knowledge to the next level by learning something about shaders and OpenGL Shading Language.

8
Adding Depth – Cinder 3D Basics

This chapter will introduce you to the basic 3D aspects and practical methods as well as the 3D primitives that can be drawn with Cinder. We will start by making a transition from 2D coordinate system to 3D, and continue with basic problems and solutions that we are going to face in the 3D graphics programming world from now on. We will also add basic animation during the walkthrough to demonstrate the basic approach of adding movement to the otherwise static objects.

Introducing the 3D space

To use Cinder with 3D we need to understand a bit about 3D computer graphics. First thing that we need to know is that 3D graphics are created in a three-dimensional space that exists somewhere in the computer and is transformed into a two-dimensional image that can be displayed on our computer screens afterwards.

Adding Depth – Cinder 3D Basics

Usually there is a projection (frustrum) that has different properties which are similar to the properties of cameras we have in the real world. **Frustrum** takes care of rendering all the 3D objects that are visible in frustrum. It is responsible for creating the 2D image that we see on the screen.

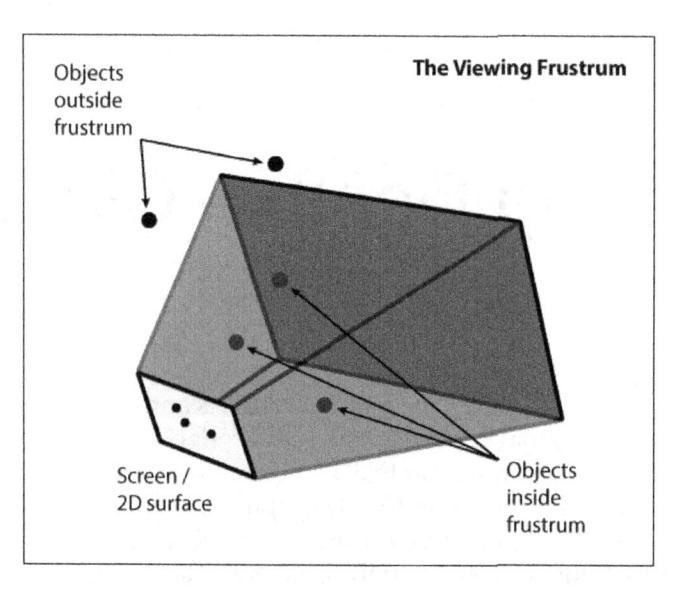

The Viewing Frustrum

- Objects outside frustrum
- Screen / 2D surface
- Objects inside frustrum

As you can see in the preceding figure, all objects inside the frustrum are being rendered on the screen. Objects outside the view frustrum are being ignored.

OpenGL (that is being used for drawing in Cinder) relies on the so called rendering pipeline to map the 3D coordinates of the objects to the 2D screen coordinates. Three kind of matrices are used for this process: the model, view, and projection matrices. The model matrix maps the 3D object's local coordinates to the world (or global) space, the view matrix maps it to the camera space, and finally the projection matrix takes care of the mapping to the 2D screen space. Older versions of OpenGL combine the model and view matrices into one – the **modelview** matrix.

In the previous chapters we used 2D coordinates (x and y coordinate axes) to place different kinds of objects and graphics on the screen. Now we will take advantage of the third dimension – the z axis.

The coordinate system in Cinder starts from the top-left corner of the screen. Any object placed there has the coordinates 0, 0, 0 (these are values of x, y, and z respectively). The x axis extends to the right, y to the bottom, but z extends towards the viewer (us), as shown in the following figure:

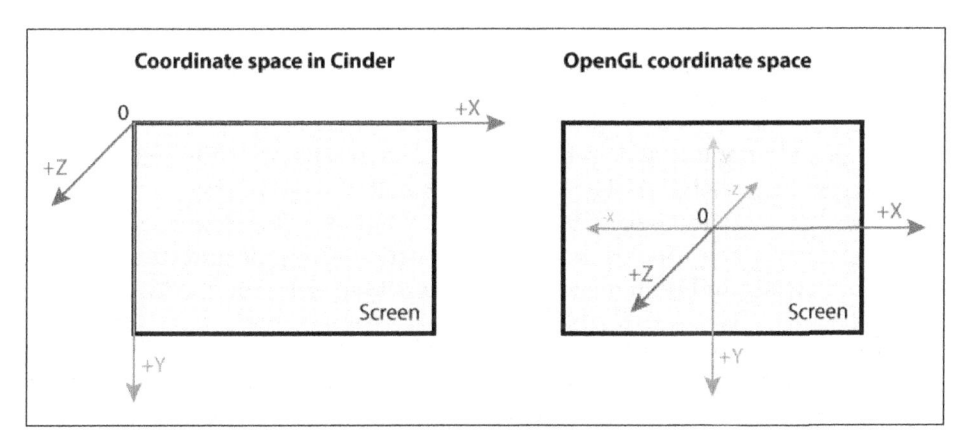

As you can see in the preceding figure, the coordinate system in Cinder is a bit different from the one in OpenGL. The built-in OpenGL drawing functions in Cinder takes care of the mapping.

Drawing in 3D

Let's try to draw something by taking into account that there is a third dimension.

Create another project by using **TinderBox** and name it Basic3D. Open the project file (xcode/Basic3D.xcodeproj on Mac or vc10\Basic3D.sln on Windows). Open Basic3DApp.cpp in the editor and navigate to the draw() method implementation.

Just after the gl::clear() method add the following line to draw a cube:

```
gl::drawCube( Vec3f(0,0,0), Vec3f(100,100,100) );
```

The first parameter defines the position of the center of the cube, the second defines its size. Note that we use the Vec3f() variables to define position and size within three (x, y and z) dimensions.

Adding Depth – Cinder 3D Basics

Compile and run the project. This will draw a solid cube at the top-left corner of the screen. We are able to see just one quarter of it because the center of the cube is the reference point. Let's move it to the center of the screen by transforming the previous line as follows:

```
gl::drawCube(
        Vec3f(getWindowWidth()/2,getWindowHeight()/2,0),
        Vec3f(100,100,100) );
```

Now we are positioning the cube in the middle of the screen no matter what the window's width or height is, because we pass half of the window's width (`getWindowWidth()/2`) and half of the window's height (`getWindowHeight()/2`) as values for the x and y coordinates of the cube's location. Compile and run the project to see the result. Play around with the size parameters to understand the logic behind it.

We may want to rotate the cube a bit. There is a built-in `rotate()` function that we can use. One of the things that we have to remember, though, is that we have to use it before drawing the object. So add the following line before `gl::drawCube()`:

```
gl::rotate( Vec3f(0,1,0) );
```

Compile and run the project. You should see a strange rotation animation around the y axis. The problem here is that the `rotate()` function rotates the whole 3D world of our application including the object in it and it does so by taking into account the scene coordinates. As the center of the 3D world (the place where all axes cross and are zero) is in the top-left corner, all rotation is happening around this point.

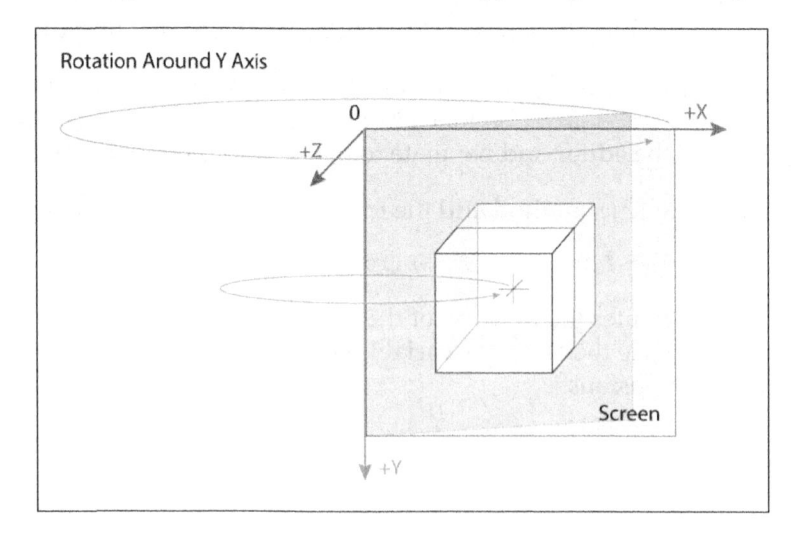

Chapter 8

To change that we have to use the `translate()` function. It is used to move the scene (or canvas) before we `rotate()` or `drawCube()`. To make our cube rotate around the center of the screen, we have to perform the following steps:

1. Use the `translate()` function to translate the 3D world to the center of the screen.
2. Use the `rotate()` function to rotate the 3D world.
3. Draw the object (`drawCube()`).
4. Use the `translate()` function to translate the scene back.

We have to use the `translate()` function to translate the scene back to the location, because each time we call `translate()` values are added instead of being replaced. In code it should look similar to the following:

```
gl::translate( Vec3f(getWindowWidth()/2,getWindowHeight()/2,0) );
gl::rotate( Vec3f::yAxis()*1 );
gl::drawCube( Vec3f::zero(), Vec3f(100,100,100) );
gl::translate( Vec3f(-getWindowWidth()/2,-getWindowHeight()/2,0) );
```

So now we get a smooth rotation of the cube around the y axis. The rotation angle around y axis is increased in each frame by 1 degree as we pass the `Vec3f::yAxis()*1` value to the `rotate()` function. Experiment with the rotation values to understand this a bit more.

What if we want the cube to be in a constant rotated position? We have to remember that the `rotate()` function works similar to the translate function. It adds values to the rotation of the scene instead of replacing them. Instead of rotating the object back, we will use the `pushMatrices()` and `popMatrices()` functions.

Rotation and translation are transformations. Every time you call `translate()` or `rotate()`, you are modifying the modelview matrix. If something is done, it is sometimes not so easy to undo it. Every time you transform something, changes are being made based on all previous transformations in the current state.

So what is this state? Each state contains a copy of the current transformation matrices. By calling `pushModelView()` we enter a fresh state by making a copy of the current modelview matrix and storing it into the stack. We will make some crazy transformations now without worrying about how we will undo them. To go back, we call `popModelView()` that pops (or deletes) the current modelview matrix from the stack, and returns us to the state with the previous modelview matrix.

Adding Depth – Cinder 3D Basics

So let's try this out by adding the following code after the `gl::clear()` call:

```
gl::pushModelView();
gl::translate( Vec3f(getWindowWidth()/2,getWindowHeight()/2,0) );
gl::rotate( Vec3f(35,20,0) );
gl::drawCube( Vec3f::zero(), Vec3f(100,100,100) );
gl::popModelView();
```

Compile and run our program now, you should see something similar to the following screenshot:

As we can see, before doing anything, we create a copy of the current state with `pushModelView()`. Then we do the same as before, translate our scene to the middle of the screen, rotate it (this time 35 degrees around x axis and 20 degrees around y axis), and finally draw the cube! To reset the stage to the state it was before, we have to use just one line of code, `popModelView()`.

Understanding nested states

It is possible to create nested states by using the previously discussed functions. By using two `pushModelView()` calls in a row, we are storing two different states. By calling one `popModelView()` afterwards, we pop just the last pushed modelview matrix.

Let's change our `draw()` method implementation to the following:

```
void Basic3DApp::draw() {
   gl::clear( Color( 0, 0, 0 ) );

   // make a copy of the current modelview matrix
   gl::pushModelView();

   // translate the origin of the world to the center of the screen
   gl::translate( Vec3f(getWindowWidth()/2,getWindowHeight()/2,0) );

   // draw a ring of cubes
```

```
        int i; // iterator
        int numCubes = 10; // number of cubes in the ring
        for ( i=0; i < numCubes; i++ )
        {
                // make another copy of the current modelview matrix
                gl::pushModelView();

                // rotate the world around z axis
                gl::rotate( Vec3f::zAxis() * (360.f / numCubes * i) );

                // draw a relatively small cube
                // 200 pixels to the right from the center of the world
                gl::drawCube( Vec3f(200,0,0), Vec3f(25,25,25) );

                // return to the previous state
                gl::popModelView();
        }

        // rotate the world around the origin
        gl::rotate( Vec3f(35,20,0) );
        // draw a bigger cube in the center of the world
        gl::drawCube( Vec3f::zero(), Vec3f(100,100,100) );
        // return to the initial state
        gl::popModelView();
}
```

Note the use of `gl::pushModelView()` and `gl::popModelView()`. Compile and run the project, you should see a ring of smaller cubes surrounding the one we saw earlier.

Now try to move the `gl::rotate()` call before the `for` loop and after the `gl::translate()` call. Compile and run the project. You should see a bit of a different image than the one you saw earlier:

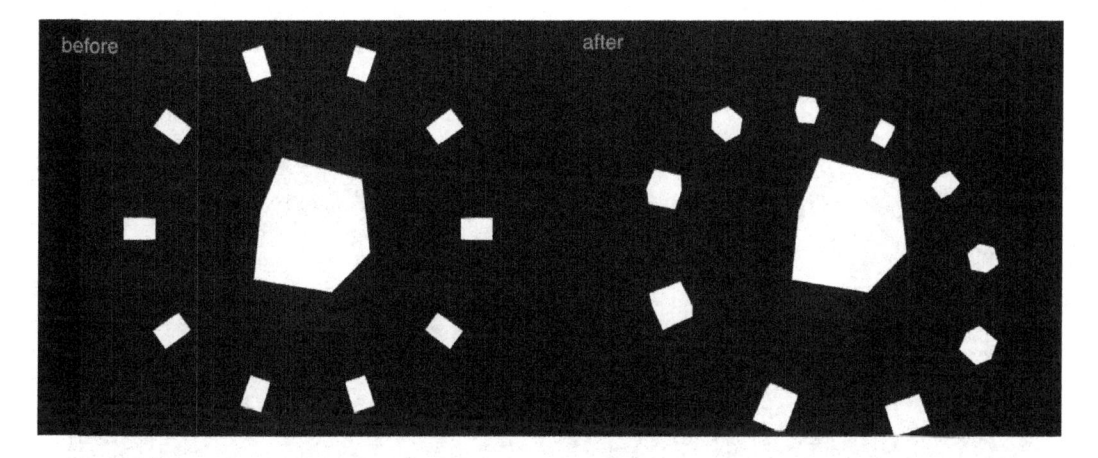

This is a simple demonstration of nested states. Try to experiment in the way we just did, by adding extra transformations and changing their order. Furthermore, OpenGL is not limited to just two levels of nested states. You could try to add orbiting objects around each of the small squares by adding more `pushModelView()` and `popModelView()` functions inside another `for` loop, for example.

Handling depth sorting

Let's take a look at the 3D primitive drawing functions that are built into Cinder. There are not a lot of them but as Cinder is meant to be a bit more low level than other similar tools, you should continue to learn some OpenGL afterwards to get the most out of Cinder and drawing in 3D space.

Let's start with changing the single colored cube into something more colorful and adding some constant rotation to it as it was before. To do that, we will have to replace the `drawCube()` function call with `drawColorCube()`:

```
gl::drawColorCube( Vec3f::zero(), Vec3f(100,100,100) );
```

When you run and compile the application, you will see that the cube is drawn somehow strange. This is the effect of inappropriate depth sorting. A 3D model consists of vertices that are placed at different depths in the current projection. These vertices form faces that also have different depth information that is taken into account when transforming them into pixels at different depths. If these vertices are not sorted and drawn in appropriate order according to their depth information, we get an image where the faces and objects behind in the back of the scene are drawn in front and the opposite. To avoid this, we have to enable the depth read feature of the OpenGL. Add these lines of code in the `setup()` method implementation:

```
gl::enableDepthRead();
```

After you compile and run the project, the cube should look just fine:

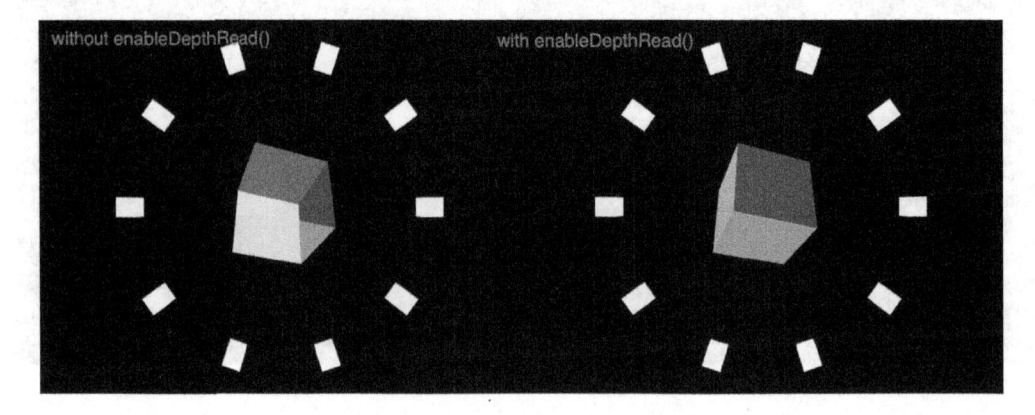

With that done, let's add some rotation animation. To do this we will need to declare some variables that will take care of storing the rotation variables. Then we will need to assign initial values to them in the `setup()` method, change them in the `update()` method, and finally draw in the `draw()` method implementation. Let's start with declaring the variables. Add these lines just after the `setup()`, `update()`, and `draw()` method declarations:

```
Vec3f currentRotation;
Vec3f rotationIncrement;
```

Instead of using one `float` variable for the current and increment rotation angle around each axis we are using the `Vec3f` datatype to be able to store the rotation values in one variable.

We have to assign the initial values to these variables now. Go to the `setup()` method implementation and add the following lines:

```
currentRotation = Vec3f( 0, 0, 0 );
rotationIncrement = Vec3f( 1.1f, 1.2f, 1.3f );
```

With that done, go to the `update()` method implementation and add the following line:

```
currentRotation += rotationIncrement;
```

This will increment the rotation around all the three axis on each frame.

Finally we have to make use of the `currentRotation` variable while drawing. Change the parameter of the `gl::rotate()` function before the `gl::drawColorCube()` call to `currentRotation` as follows:

```
...
// rotate the world around the origin
gl::rotate( currentRotation );

// draw a bigger cube in the center
gl::drawColorCube( Vec3f::zero(), Vec3f(100,100,100) );
```

Now the rotation values will be increased and updated on each frame. Compile and run the project to see for yourself! You should get a nice rotation animation. Try to do the same with the location and size of the cube for better understanding of how this works.

Adding Depth – Cinder 3D Basics

Exploring other Cinder 3D primitives

Now let's try out the different 3D primitives that Cinder supplies it's own functions for. We just tried to draw a different kind of cube, so let's continue with something equally classic, a sphere. Replace the `gl::drawColorCube()` function call with the following line:

```
gl::drawSphere( Vec3f::zero(), 100 );
```

The first parameter of this function defines the center of the sphere and the second defines the radius. There is a third (optional) parameter `int` that controls the number of segments the sphere is made of. The default value is 12, but you might want to change it to a higher value to increase the smoothness of the sphere.

Compile and run the project. You should see an image similar to the following screenshot:

The problem here is that it does not look quite 3D. As you might have already guessed, the problem is that there is no light. To add light to the scene, add the following lines in the `setup()` method implementation:

```
glEnable( GL_LIGHTING );
glEnable( GL_LIGHT0 );
```

These are OpenGL functions that are responsible for turning the light on. The first one enables light as such, the second is turning on the first light or `GL_LIGHT0`. There are ways of positioning and changing it's parameters, but we won't dig into this as it is outside the scope of this book.

Compile and run the project to see the sphere with lights turned on. You should get a result that is similar to the following screenshot:

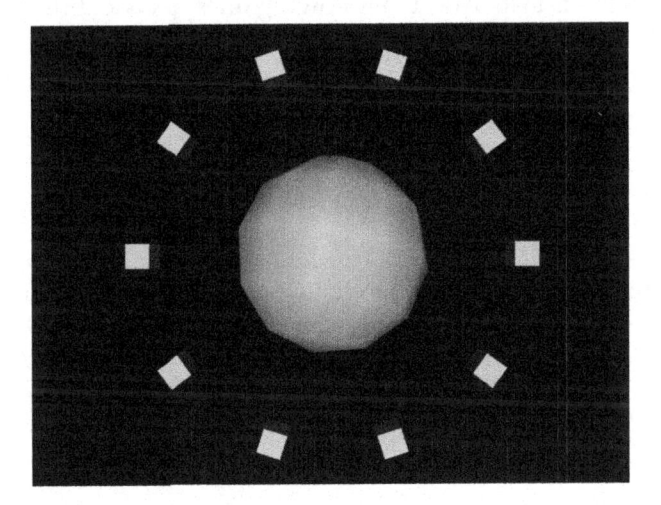

Let's try to draw something else instead of a sphere. How about a cylinder? Replace the `drawSphere()` function call with the following line:

```
gl::drawCylinder(50, 50, 100);
```

This will draw an open-ended cylinder on the screen. The first parameter defines the width of the cylinder base, the second parameter defines the width of the cylinder top. The third parameter defines the cylinder height.

After we compile and run the application, you will notice that the cylinder is not rotating around it's center like the cube or sphere we drew before. That is because of the way it is drawn – from the bottom up instead of both – up and down. To change that, we can draw another cylinder, with a negative height or change the `translate()` values. For the sake of simplicity, let's draw another cylinder. Replace the cylinder drawing code to this:

```
gl::drawCylinder(50, 50, 50);
gl::drawCylinder(50, 50, -50);
```

Adding Depth – Cinder 3D Basics

We can see the same cylinder but now it rotates around its center. Another thing that we might want to add are the closed ends of the cylinder. We have to use 2D shapes again to accomplish this task. Add the following lines of code directly after the `drawCylinder()` function calls:

```
gl::rotate( Vec3f(-90,0,0) );
gl::translate( Vec3f(0,0,50) );
gl::drawSolidCircle(Vec2f(0,0), 50, 12);
gl::translate( Vec3f(0,0,-50) );
gl::rotate( Vec3f(180,0,0) );
gl::translate( Vec3f(0,0,50) );
```

gl::drawSolidCircle(Vec2f(0,0), 50, 12); Not too easy, right? There is no `drawSolidCircle()` function that would draw a circle based on 3D coordinates yet, but this is a kind of shorthand anyway so we don't have to write pure OpenGL. What these lines of code do is that they move the scene or canvas in appropriate position and rotation relative to the already drawn cylinder to draw the top and the bottom of it.

Let's change the code a bit, so we see another thing that is possible with the `drawCylinder()` function that is drawing a cone or even a pyramid:

```
gl::drawCylinder(50, 0, 50, 4);
gl::drawCylinder(50, 0, -50, 4);
```

Delete or comment out the `drawSolidCircle()` part and change the top values of the `drawCylinder()` functions to 0 and add a fourth value (and set it to 4 or more if you want to draw a cone) that represents the slice count of the cylinder.

After compiling and running the application, a pyramid is not quite what we see. Let's call it a diamond to describe the shape more correctly. In the following screenshot you can see an image strip with the `gl::drawCylinder()` adjustments we just did:

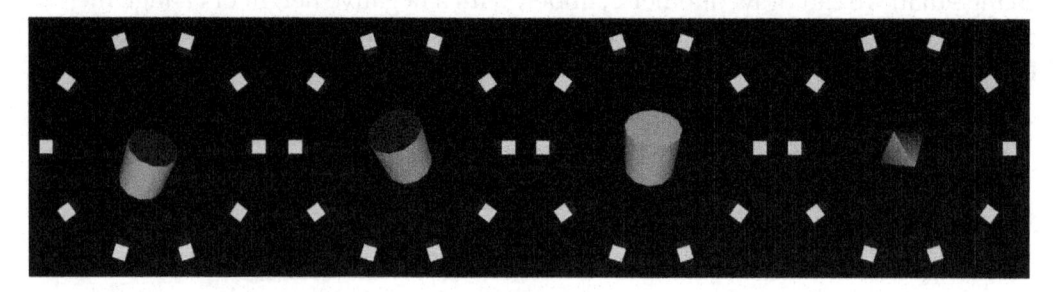

Another basic shape worth introducing is the torus. Cinder has a built-in function for drawing this and this is how the function looks:

```
gl::drawTorus(100, 20);
```

Add the preceding line of code after the cylinder drawing function calls. The first parameter defines the outer radius (the circle responsible for the base shape of the torus), the second defines the inner radius or the radius if the circle that is used for creating the volume of the torus.

To make things look even more straightedged, let's add the third and fourth parameter that are responsible for the longitude and latitude segment count of the torus:

```
gl::drawTorus(100, 20, 8, 8);
```

If we compile and run the application now, we should see an image similar to one of these:

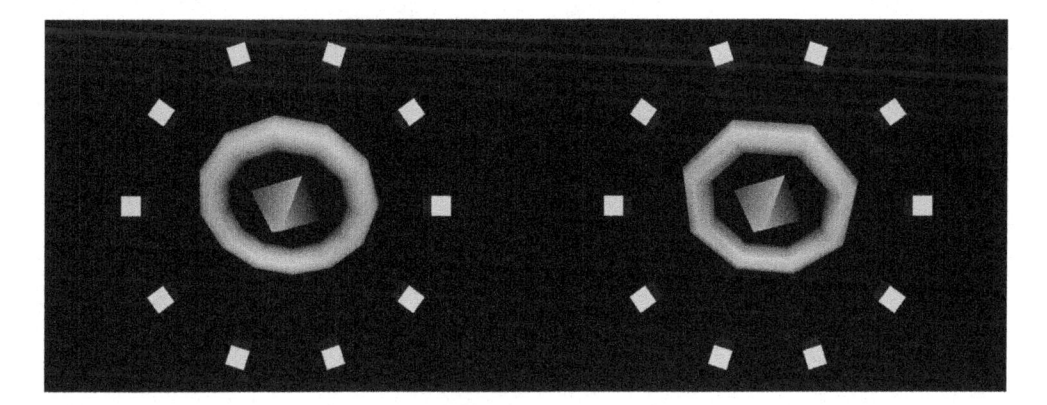

Summary

To sum up, in this chapter we introduced ourselves with the very basic 3D stuff that can be done with Cinder. We understood a bit about the concept of 3D space as well as how to draw and animate objects in this space. We learned to switch on the lightning and construct more complex shapes out of primitives.

There is more, but to get the real graphics power out of Cinder, you have to learn some more of OpenGL and the **OpenGL Shading Language** (**GLSL**).

In the next chapter, we will talk less about graphics but more about what is possible with Cinder in terms of audio.

9
Enter Sound – Adding Sound and Audio

In this chapter, we will talk a bit about the concept of sound in creative coding.

In this chapter we will learn the following:

- How to load and play sound in Cinder
- How to modify sound in real time
- How to use audio data to draw and animate
- How to make use of live sound input

Loading and playing a sound file

There are several ways of using sound in creative coding. One way is to use audio samples, another one is to use live input, and then there is the possibility of generating sound from scratch. Nevertheless, a lot more possibilities emerge when you start to combine all of these approaches.

In this chapter, we will learn to load, play, and visualize audio files and capture live input. To get started, open TinderBox and make another project with the name `BasicAudio`. Open `xcode/BasicAudio.xcodeproj` (`vc10\BasicAudio.sln` on Windows). Open `BasicAudioApp.cpp` in the editor.

To use the basic audio features of Cinder, we have to import the appropriate libraries:

```
#include "cinder/audio/Output.h"
```

This particular one contains all the code that is needed to load and play back an audio file. Go and find your own audio file (`mp3` or `wav` will work), and place it in the project's `assets` folder.

Enter Sound – Adding Sound and Audio

We will need an `audio::SourceRef` object for storing the reference to the audio source that we will use in our code. Add the following line to your class declaration:

```
audio::SourceRef src;
```

Add the following code snippet into the `setup()` method implementation:

```
src = audio::load(loadAsset("sample.wav"));
audio::Output::play(src);
```

This will load the audio file into the computer memory as the `audio::Source` object and save a reference in the `src` variable. Then, we can play the sound by using the `audio::Output::play()` class method.

Compile and run our application. You should hear the sound. There are some limitations with this way of playing the sound back. It is not possible to apply the loop control to it in any other way (except for setting and getting the volume).

Using tracks

The Cinder `Track` class provides more control over a sound file. Let's go over a couple of features of the `Track` class that we might use most often.

To loop the loaded audio file, we will need to add a `Track` object to the `Output` object and save the returned track reference so that we can use it to control the sound later. Add a variable for storing the track reference in the class declaration:

```
audio::TrackRef trackRef;
```

Replace the code in the `setup()` method implementation with the following:

```
src = audio::load(loadAsset("sample.wav"));
trackRef = audio::Output::addTrack(src);
```

This will basically do the same as before for now, except that it will store the `audio::Source` pointer as a separate track in the `audio::Output` object. The `addTrack()` function has another parameter, `autoplay`, which is automatically set to `true` if we don't provide the other value. Let's try to set it to `false`:

```
trackRef = audio::Output::addTrack(src, false);
```

As we set the `autoplay` parameter to `false`, audio file is not played after it is loaded. We can use this approach if we want the audio file to be played at some other point of the application flow. Use the following code to play it:

```
trackRef->play();
```

We used the arrow syntax here because the track reference is just a C++ pointer to the actual `Track` object. All other properties of the track are accessed in the same manner.

We can add more than one track to the `Output` object by creating a new audio source object and adding it to the `audio::Output` pointer. We won't do it now, but keep in mind that this is possible in case we want to create some kind of multilayer audio application.

Changing track parameters

Next thing that we want to do is to make the audio file play again after it has finished playing. It is possible by setting the looping of the track to `true`:

```
trackRef->setLooping(true);
```

This will make the track loop infinite.

Another thing that we might want to do is to change the track volume. You can think of the `Output` volume as the master volume and the `Track` volumes as individual track volumes of a mixer.

To change the volume, use the following code:

```
trackRef->setVolume(0.5f); // set track volume
audio::Output::setVolume(0.5f); // set master volume
```

We can use variables to dynamically change the volume of the sound. Let's do that for both master and track volumes.

Add the following lines to the class declaration of the app:

```
float masterVol, trackVol;
void mouseMove(MouseEvent event);
```

With these lines of code, we declare two floats that will store the master and track volumes and a `mouseMove` method override of the `AppBasic` class that will let us respond to mouse movements.

Enter Sound – Adding Sound and Audio

Let's go to the `setup()` method implementation and initialize the `masterVol` and `trackVol` variables, additionally change the raw values of `trackRef->setVolume()` and `audio::Output::setVolume()`:

```
void BasicAudioApp::setup() {
  masterVol = trackVol = 0.5f;
  src = audio::load(loadAsset("sample.wav"));
  trackRef = audio::Output::addTrack(src, false);
  trackRef->setLooping(true);
  trackRef->setVolume(trackVol); // set track volume
  audio::Output::setVolume(masterVol); // set master volume
  trackRef->play();
}
```

Add the implementation of the `mouseMove` method at the end of the file, before the `CINDER_APP_BASIC()` call:

```
void BasicAudioApp::mouseMove(MouseEvent event) {
    masterVol = (float)event.getX()/getWindowWidth();
    trackVol = (float)event.getY()/getWindowHeight();
    audio::Output::setVolume(masterVol);
    trackRef->setVolume(trackVol);
}
```

An `event` object of the type `MouseEvent` is passed to this method. We can get the current location of the mouse cursor at the time of the event as well as many other parameters that the `event` object holds. We will stick to the mouse x and y coordinates for now and use them for changing the volume.

For changing the master volume, we are using the x coordinate. We are using the y coordinate for the track volume.

As volume of the sound in Cinder is defined in a range from `0.0f` to `1.0f`, we need to transform the mouse positions in this kind of form. To do that, we need to divide the actual mouse position with its maximum range that is the width and height of the window. So, if the mouse x position is `0` and window width is `100`, after dividing the coordinate with the window width (0/100) we get `0`. If the mouse x position is `100`, we get `1`. Additionally, if the mouse x position is `50`, we get `0.5` (50/100).

As the mouse positions and window dimensions are returned as `int` values, we will need to cast one of the values to `float` for a successful floating point number operation. That is why there is `(float)` before the `event.getX()/getWindowWidth()` and `event.getY()/getWindowHeight()` parts of the code, it casts the `int` value returned by `event.getX()` to `float`. Finally, we set the master volume and track volume with `audio::Output::setVolume(masterVol);` and `trackRef->setVolume(trackVol);`.

Compile and run our application. Move the mouse, you should hear how the volume of the sound is changing.

Next useful feature that we might want to learn is jumping to a certain position of the time of the track. To do that, we will use the `mouseDrag` method of the `AppBasic` class. Let's declare an override of it by adding the following line to the class declaration:

```
void mouseDrag(MouseEvent event);
```

Let's implement that. Add the following code at the end of the file, before the `CINDER_APP_BASIC()` call:

```
void BasicAudioApp::mouseDrag(MouseEvent event) {
    double time =
    (double)event.getX()/getWindowWidth()*src->getDuration();
    trackRef->setTime( time );
}
```

In this example, the application window's width is being mapped to the duration of the track. The x position of the mouse is being transformed to a specific time in the audio track. The `trackRef->setTime(time)` part of the code sets the position of the track playhead.

Compile and run our application. You should be able to do live seeking now. Click and drag to try that out.

Visualizing audio

There is one important thing missing in our creative sound application—the visual side of it. Let's create a simple equalizer.

First, we will need to enable the PCM buffering of the audio track.

PCM stands for **pulse code modulation** and it is a method for digitally representing sampled analog signals. An analog audio signal is the fluctuation of voltage inside a conductor. A digital representation of that are samples or bytes with floating point values usually from `-1` to `1`.

In the world of audio sampling there is a term, sampling rate, which represents the amount of samples or values being sampled each second. The PCM values and sampling rate of an audio file determine its playback speed.

Enter Sound – Adding Sound and Audio

To enable PCM buffering and be able to read PCM values during application runtime, add the following code in the `setup()` method's declaration before `trackRef->play()`:

```
trackRef->enablePcmBuffering( true );
```

Second, we need a variable that will serve as a pointer to the track's PCM buffer.

A PCM buffer is the secret place in computer memory where the raw values of the sound wave coming out from our speakers reside. Before any sound is sent to the audio output, it is kept in the buffer for some time. When the sound is played, the buffer is cleared and filled again with new audio data.

We will need to access the PCM buffer to read the raw waveform values from it. Add the following line to the class declaration to add a variable that will serve as a reference to it:

```
audio::PcmBuffer32fRef pcmBuffer;
```

Third, we need to get a copy of the most recent buffer in each frame. Add the following code to the `update()` method implementation:

```
pcmBuffer = trackRef->getPcmBuffer();
```

Finally, change the `draw()` method implementation as follows:

```
void BasicAudioApp::draw() {
  // clear the screen by drawing
  // a semi-transparent black rectangle all over the screen
  gl::enableAlphaBlending();
  gl::color( 0.f, 0.f, 0.f, 0.1f );
  gl::drawSolidRect(getWindowBounds());

  if( !pcmBuffer ) {
    gl::disableAlphaBlending();
    return; // stop here if the buffer is empty
  }

  // get copy of the left channel data from the pcmBuffer
  audio::Buffer32fRef buffer =
  pcmBuffer->getChannelData( audio::CHANNEL_FRONT_LEFT );

  // get buffer length
  uint32_t bufferLength = pcmBuffer->getSampleCount();

  // calculate scale for mapping the buffer data on the screen
  float scale = getWindowWidth() / (float)bufferLength;
```

```
    // set color to cyan
    gl::color( 0.f, 1.f ,1.f ,0.8f );

    // loop through current buffer data
    // in steps of 10 and construct waveform
    for( int i=0; i<bufferLength; i+=10 ) {
      // map current x position of buffer value to window width
      float x = i * scale;

      // buffer data fluctuates from -1 to +1,
      // map it to window height
      float y = ( (buffer->mData[i]+1) * getWindowHeight()/2 );

      // draw a circle
      gl::drawStrokedCircle( Vec2f(x, y),
        ( abs(buffer->mData[i])*getWindowHeight()/2 ) );
    }

    gl::disableAlphaBlending();
}
```

Compile and run our application, you should see an image as shown in the following screenshot:

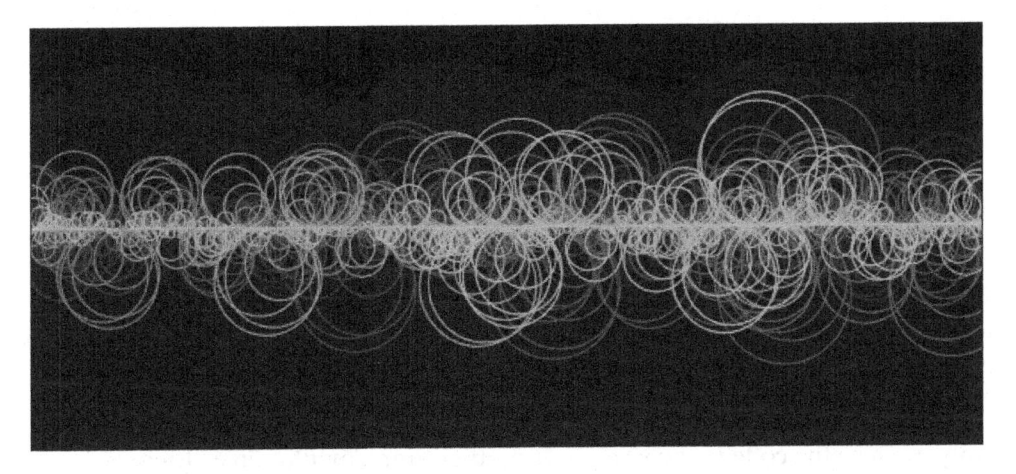

Using audio input

How about using a microphone or line-in as the audio source? No problem. To make this possible, we will need to import the audio `Input` library:

```
#include "cinder/audio/Input.h"
```

We are going to extend our current application so that we can switch between live input and playback of the loaded file. We will need to declare two new variables for this:

```
audio::Input input;
bool useInput;
```

The first variable represents our sound input, and we will use the second one as a switch.

Next, we have to initialize the `input` variable, so go to the `setup()` method implementation and add the following line there:

```
input = audio::Input();
```

This assigns the default audio input to the `input` variable.

Let's use the `mouseDown` method override and fill it with the following code:

```
useInput = !useInput;

if ( useInput ) {
    input.start();
    trackRef->stop();
} else {
    input.stop();
    trackRef->play();
}
```

These lines of code handle the switching between live and loaded input. Every time the mouse is clicked, the `useInput` variable is inverted from `false` to `true` or vice versa. Depending on the value we get, we enable the live or loaded input.

Finally, replace the code in the `update()` method implementation as follows:

```
if ( useInput ) pcmBuffer = input.getPcmBuffer();
else pcmBuffer = trackRef->getPcmBuffer();
```

These lines of code get the current PCM buffer. If the `useInput` variable is set to `true`, we use the PCM buffer of the live input, if not, we use the PCM buffer of the loaded track.

Compile and run the application. Click on the window to enable live input. Click again to return to the loaded sound.

Summary

In this chapter we learned the basics of audio in Cinder. We learned how to load and play back an audio file, how to change its volume, and seek and visualize the PCM buffer. We also learned how to use live input audio data.

With this knowledge, now we are able to create audio-reactive applications that are capable of analyzing almost any kind of sound in real time and provide high performance visual feedback. Audio analysis is a broad topic and you may want to study it further. Try to Google "FFT", "octave analysis", or "beat tracking", for example. It is also possible to use some kind of third-party audio processing library, if the features that Cinder provides in terms of audio processing are not enough for you.

10
Talk to the User – Adding Interactivity and UI Events

In this chapter we will learn the following topics:

- Detecting a key press on the keyboard
- Detecting mouse movement and clicks
- Creating an application that will use basic input for real-time control

We have used some of these functionality in the previous chapters, but here we will try to gain a more systematic overview of what kind of basic interactivity is possible with Cinder.

Handling events

Throughout this book we are writing a code that basically extends the functionality of the `cinder::app::AppBasic` class and base class `App` that it inherits. The methods that we are declaring and implementing are basically overrides of virtual functions that are built in the `AppBasic` and `App` classes and are called upon in certain events. Some of them can be called event handlers, and what they basically do is they respond to certain events that are happening during the application flow.

There are three basic methods that form the core of a Cinder application:

- `setup()`
- `update()`
- `draw()`

Talk to the User – Adding Interactivity and UI Events

These methods handle the events that are happening inside the application core and a user can't control whether these functions are called or not (it is possible to stop the execution of the method by using `return` or similar means at the beginning of the function implementation).

Then there are methods that can be used to execute code on certain events for example moving your mouse, pressing a key on the keyboard, scrolling the mouse wheel, and so on. These are the ones we will focus on during this chapter. So here is a list of methods (or event handlers) that we will override:

- `keyDown()`
- `keyUp()`
- `fileDrop()`
- `mouseDown()`
- `mouseUp()`
- `mouseMove()`
- `mouseDrag()`

Let's create a simple drawing application that will use all of these events. To do so, we will need to create a new project. Open **TinderBox** and create a new project with the name `BasicEvents`. Open the project file (`xcode/BasicEvents.xcodeproj` on Mac OS X or `vc10\BasicEvents.sln` on Windows). Open the `BasicEventsApp.cpp` in the editor and let's start to add some code there.

Using mouseMove()

First we will add a custom mouse cursor that will fall down slowly while we don't move the mouse, and returns to the current mouse position when we move it. To do so we have to declare objects that will hold the x and y position of the cursor. Add the following line of code to the class declaration part of the file:

```
Vec2i cursorPos;
```

This variable will hold the x and y positions of our cursor as `int` values. The `i` part of the `Vec2i` tells us that it is a two-dimensional vector that consists of integer values.

Next we need to initialize the value by setting it to the current mouse position at the application launch. Add the following line of code to the `setup()` method implementation:

```
cursorPos = getMousePos();
```

This will get the current mouse position and assign it to our cursor position value.

Next, we want to draw a circle at the `cursorPos` coordinates. Let's navigate to the `draw()` method implementation of our application and add the following line just after the `gl::clear()` function call:

```
gl::drawSolidCircle( cursorPos, 10 );
```

We've used this function before. This will draw a circle with the radius of 10 pixels at the position defined by the `cursorPos` variable. Compile and run the project to see for yourself!

Next we want to add the falling motion to the circle. To do so, we will need to update the circle's y position by each frame. In other words, we are going to increase the y coordinate of the circle by one frame each. Let's navigate to the `update()` method implementation and add a simple line of code as follows:

```
cursorPos.y++;
```

This will let our cursor fall down. Finally we need to make it stick to the mouse on the `mouseMove` event. We will need to declare the `mouseMove()` method override in the class declaration of our application. Add the following line at the end of the class declaration:

```
void mouseMove(MouseEvent event);
```

And the method implementation to the class implementation as follows:

```
void BasicEventsApp::mouseMove(MouseEvent event) {
    cursorPos = event.getPos();
}
```

There is more than one way of getting the current mouse position and instead of `event.getPos()`. We could use `getMousePos()` and it would do the same thing that is assigned to the mouse position to the `cursorPos` variable.

Talk to the User – Adding Interactivity and UI Events

Compile and run our application to see the result as shown in the following screenshot:

You should see a falling circle that sticks to the mouse as you move it.

Using mouseDown()

The next event handler that we are going to implement is the `mouseDown()` handler. It will execute code every time we click on any of the mouse buttons. We will write code that will add a static circle on the screen every time we click the left mouse button. It will remove the first circle when we click the right mouse button.

To begin with, we will need to declare a new variable that will be able to store more than one pair of coordinates for our generated circles. We could use an array of `Vec2i` objects but as we don't know the exact count of the circles we are going to create, we will use a C++ `vector`.

A **vector** is a dynamic array that is able to store `std::vector::max_size` amount of objects of a certain type. A `vector` array changes it's size (or length) dynamically on element add (or push) and remove (or pop).

Add the following lines of code at the end of our class declaration:

```
vector<Vec2i> circlePositions;
void mouseDown(MouseEvent event);
```

It is possible that the `mouseDown()` method is declared for us already. If so, don't mention the second line of the code. If `mouseDown()` was not declared before, go ahead and add the event handler method to the class implementation:

```cpp
void BasicEventsApp::mouseDown(MouseEvent event)
{
    // check if the left mouse button was pressed
    if ( event.isLeft() ) {
        // it was
        Vec2i cp = event.getPos(); // save current mouse position
        circlePositions.push_back(cp); // and add it to the vector
    }

    // check if the right mouse button was pressed
    if ( event.isRight() ) {
        // it was
        // check if the vector has at least one element
        if ( !circlePositions.empty() ) {
            // it has, erase the first element
            circlePositions.erase(circlePositions.begin());
        }
    }
}
```

As you can tell from the comments in the preceding code, it checks which mouse button has been pressed and then decides what to do next. As we stated before, a circle has to be created when you click the left-mouse button and a circle has to be removed when you click on the right-mouse button. Actually we do not create circles here, we just save their positions. In the `draw()` method we will be able to chose whether we want to draw circles or something else entirely.

So let's navigate to the `draw()` method implementation and add the following code snippet:

```cpp
// declare an iterator for this specific kind of vector
vector<Vec2i>::iterator i;

// loop through circle positions
for ( i=circlePositions.begin(); i!=circlePositions.end(); ++i ) {
    // and draw circles at these positions one by one
    gl::drawSolidCircle( *i, 20 );
}
```

Talk to the User – Adding Interactivity and UI Events

To loop through a vector we have to use an iterator in this case. Vector iterators are objects that are designed to traverse the vector. In this case the iterator object is like a pointer and a `vector<Vec2i>` type iterator will point to a `Vec2i` object inside of it. By increasing and decreasing the iterator position we gain access to the next or previous item in the vector. It is possible to get the `begin()` and `end()` iterators from a vector and they point to the first and the past-the-end element of a vector respectively.

To access an element through the iterator (that is similar to a pointer), we have to make use of the concept of **dereferencing**. To dereference a pointer we have to use an asterisk (*) before the pointer variable. If `i` is a pointer to the actual position of a circle, to access the actual `Vec2i` object that stores the coordinates, we have to use `*i`. To access properties of the object, we write `(*i).x` or `i->x`.

Compile and run the project. You should be able to add and remove circles by clicking on the right and left buttons of your mouse.

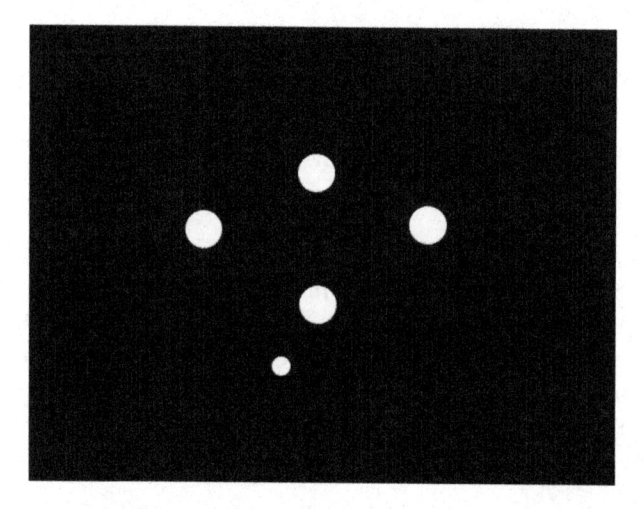

You can do the same by using the `mouseUp()` event handler instead of `mouseDown()`. The only difference is that the code will be executed when you release the mouse button.

Using mouseDrag()

Next we are going to make use of the `mouseDrag()` event handler to draw a polyline on the screen. We will need another `vector` for storing the coordinates of the points that will actually form the polyline. Let's declare the `vector` and `mouseDrag()` event handlers in the class declaration. Add the following line of code at the end of it:

```
PolyLine<Vec2f> line;
void mouseDrag(MouseEvent event);
```

We use `PolyLine<Vec2f>` here because `PolyLine` is a Cinder class that is used to store control point values of a line. We use `Vec2f` instead of `int`, because there is no `draw` function in Cinder that would accept a `PolyLine` class that consists of `int` values.

Let's move to the next step and add the implementation of the `mouseDrag()` method to the class implementation:

```
void BasicEventsApp::mouseDrag(MouseEvent event) {
    // create new position from current mouse position
    Vec2f cp = event.getPos();

    // copy it to the PolyLine
    line.push_back(cp);
}
```

This will add a new position with the current mouse coordinates to the `PolyLine` each time a change in mouse position is detected.

Lastly, we have to draw the `PolyLine`. So let's navigate to the `draw()` method implementation and add the following line of code there:

```
if ( line.size() ) {
  gl::drawSolid(line);
}
```

The `gl::drawSolid` function will basically draw a filled polygon. The `PolyLine` itself defines the outline of the polygon. Compile and run the project to see what I mean to say. You should end up with an image similar to the one shown in the following screenshot:

If you want to draw a line, use `gl::draw(line)` instead.

Talk to the User – Adding Interactivity and UI Events

Using keyDown()

It would be nice if we had the ability to clear the screen while the application is running instead of closing and reopening it to start again. Let's make use of the `keyDown()` event handler to detect a key press. What we want to do is to erase all circles and the line when the C key is pressed. To do that, we need to declare the `keyDown()` method in the class declaration:

```
void keyDown(KeyEvent event);
```

Next we have to implement this, so add the following code snippet at the end of the file:

```
void BasicEventsApp::keyDown(KeyEvent event) {
    if ( event.getCode() == KeyEvent::KEY_c ) {
        circlePositions.clear();
        line.getPoints().clear();
    }
}
```

The `keyDown()` method takes a `KeyEvent` parameter that contains the code of the key that is being pressed. Here we check if the key code represents the letter C on the keyboard and if that is `true`, we clear the `circlePositions` vector and vector values in the `PolyLine` object that actually stores the control points in the same manner as the `vector circlePositions` does.

You can do the same thing with the `keyUp()` event handler. We won't make a separate example of it now as it works exactly the same way when a key is released.

Using fileDrop()

What we will do though is we will make use of the `fileDrop()` event handler to place a picture in the background. It takes `FileDropEvent` object as a parameter. It contains the path to the file that is being dropped on to the application window. To make use of that path, we need to add these lines at the top of the class file:

```
#include "cinder/gl/Texture.h"
#include "cinder/ImageIo.h"
```

The first include is needed because it contains the `gl::Texture` class that we will need in order to store the background image and to draw it by using the `gl::draw()` function. The `ImageIo.h` file is here because of the image loading functions that we will need to load an actual image into the `Texture` instance.

Next, we need to declare a variable that will store the background image and the `fileDrop()` event method itself. Add the following lines of code at the end of the class declaration:

```
gl::Texture background;
void fileDrop(FileDropEvent);
```

Now we need to implement the `fileDrop()` method. Add the following lines of code in the class implementation:

```
void BasicEventsApp::fileDrop(FileDropEvent event) {
    try {
        background = gl::Texture( loadImage( event.getFile(0) ) );
    } catch( ... ) {
        console() << "unable to load file" << endl;
    };
}
```

Here we are making use of the `try` and `catch` statement. By doing this we just make sure that our application does not crash if the wrong kind of file is being dropped. We load an image into the `background` variable if we are lucky or print an error message to the console if not.

Take a closer look on the `console()` function call. The `console()` function refers to the standard output or console. This is one of the best debugging tools in the world and you should consider using it if you are not using it already.

There is one last thing missing, we have to draw the `background`. Go to the `draw()` method implementation and add the following code snippet right after the `gl::clear()` function call and before all the code we added to this method during this chapter. We do so because the background is the first thing that we need to draw in each frame:

```
if ( background ) {
    gl::draw( background, getWindowBounds() );
}
```

Before we draw a texture, we have to make sure that it actually exists. That's why we are using an extra if statement. Only then 'can' we draw the background texture within the bounds of our application window that is returned by the `getWindowBounds()` method call.

Compile and run our application. Drop an image file on to the window of our application and see what happens. You should see an image similar to the following screenshot:

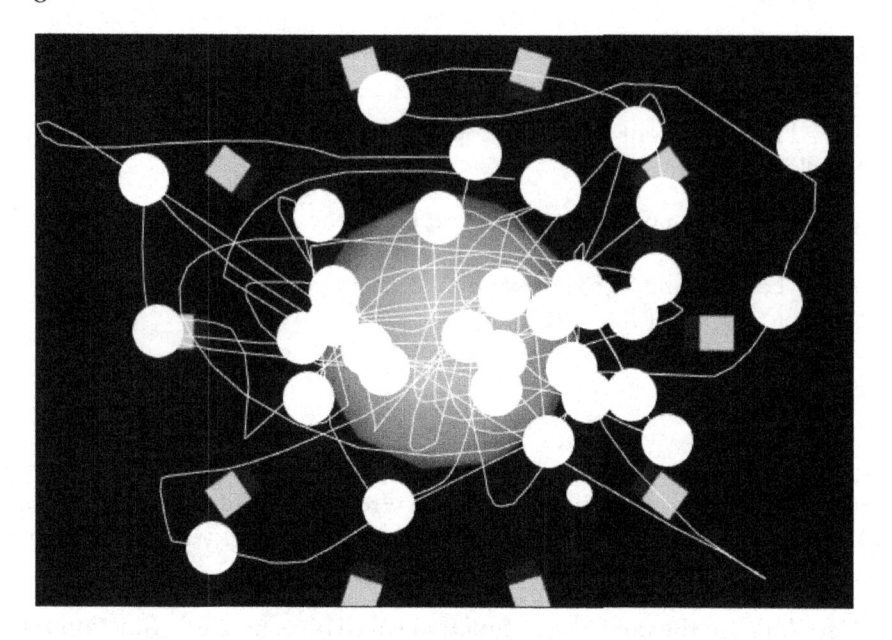

Summary

In this chapter, we gained a basic understanding about the built-in and mostly used events that any kind of application could make use of. We learned how to make use of mouse press, mouse drag, key press, and even file drop events. We also made use of some new drawing methods that were not explained in previous chapters.

In the next chapter, we are going to talk about communication between applications built-in Cinder, and other applications on the same or other networked computer by using Syphon and Open Sound Control message system.

Basic Cinder Functionality Reference

This part of the book will help you find some basic Cinder functionalities used in this book for later reference. This reference is very basic, so if you are an experienced developer searching for detailed and in-depth function reference, you should take a look at the reference on the Cinder website (http://libcinder.org), or as Cinder is open-source, at the actual source code of Cinder.

Basic types

These are the basic types consumed by many other Cinder functions. This assumes that you are already familiar with `int`, `float`, and other basic data types in C++.

```
cinder::Vec2f( float x, float y )
```

The preceding code represents a two-dimensional vector of `float` values (x and y). This is usually used to represent location or size in two-dimensional space.

```
cinder::Vec2i( int x, int y )
```

The preceding code represents a two-dimensional vector of `int` values (x and y). This is usually used to represent location or size in two-dimensional space.

```
cinder::Vec3f( float x, float y, float z )
```

The preceding code represents a three-dimensional vector of `float` values (x, y, and z). This is usually used to represent location or size in three-dimensional space.

```
cinder::Rectf( float x1, float y1, float x2, float y2 )
```

The preceding code represents an abstract rectangle that is defined by the top-left and bottom-right corner coordinates.

```
cinder::Color( float r, float g, float b, float a )
```

In the preceding code, the Color object or class represents color in the Cinder environment—`r` is for red, `g` is for green, `b` is for blue, and `a` is for alpha in range form `0.0f` to `1.0f`.

Applications

The following functions form the base of your Cinder application:

- `setup()`
- `update()`
- `draw()`

We use `setup()` for the preparation, `update()` for calculations in the run loop, and `draw()` for drawing on the screen. You can use the `shutdown()` method to do something (clear memory, store data, or communicate with remote server) before our application closes. Remember that your main Cinder application class should derive from the `BaseApp` class and that you should implement the methods in the class declaration first.

```
void YourApp::setup() {
  // setup goes here
}

void YourApp::update() {
  // prepare data
}

void YourApp::draw() {
  // draw
}
void YourApp::shutdown() {
  // do something before the app closes
}
```

If you want to change the initial window size or other initial parameters of the application, use the `prepareSettings()` method (do not forget to declare this method first):

```
void YourApp::prepareSettings( Settings * settings ) {
  settings->setWindowSize( 800, 600 ); // set window to 800x600 px
}
```

Then, there are a couple of useful functions that you can use during setup and runtime.

`cinder::app::getWindowWidth()`

The preceding function returns the application window width as an `int` value.

`cinder::app::getWindowHeight()`

The preceding function returns the application window height as an `int` value.

`cinder::app::getWindowSize()`

The preceding function returns the application window size as a `Vec2i` value.

`cinder::app::getFrameRate()`

Sometimes, it is necessary to know the current frame rate of the application. The preceding function returns it as a `float` value.

`cinder::app::getElapsedSeconds()`

The preceding function returns the number of seconds that have passed since the application has started as a `double` value.

`cinder::app::getElapsedFrames()`

The preceding function returns the number of frames that have elapsed since the start of the application as an `int` value.

`console()`

Use the preceding function for debugging, for example, `console() << "debug text" << std::endl;`.

`isFullScreen()`

The preceding function returns `true`, if the application is in the `fullscreen` mode, `false` if not.

`setFullScreen( bool fullScreen )`

Basic Cinder Functionality Reference

The preceding code sets the `fullscreen` state by passing `true` or `false`.

To make these functions work, you have to import the `AppBasic` header file as follows:

```
#include "cinder/app/AppBasic.h"
```

Basic graphics

These functions are usually used within the `draw()` method implementation.

```
cinder::gl::clear( Color color )
```

The preceding code clears the screen with the color specified in `Color`.

```
cinder::gl::drawLine( Vec2f from, Vec2f to )
```

The preceding code draws a line from a point defined in `from` to a point defined in `to`.

```
cinder::gl::color( float r, float g, float b, float a )
```

The preceding code sets the color that is then used in drawing shapes and lines. Color is defined as the separate `r`, `g`, `b`, and `a` (optional) float values.

```
cinder::glLineWidth( float width )
```

The preceding code sets the line width of Cinder line drawing functions.

```
cinder::gl::drawSolidCircle( Vec2f center, float radius, int numSegments = 0 )
```

The preceding code draws filled circle at the position defined in `center` and radius defined in `radius`.

```
cinder::gl::drawStrokedCircle( Vec2f center, float radius, int numSegments = 0 )
```

The preceding code draws just the outline of a circle whose position is defined in `center` and radius in `radius`.

```
cinder::gl::drawSolidRect( Rectf rect )
```

The preceding code draws a solid filled rectangle that is defined in `rect`.

```
cinder::gl::drawStrokedRect( Rectf rect )
```

[124]

The preceding code draws an outline of a rectangle defined in `rect`.

```
cinder::gl::drawSolidEllipse( Vec2f position, float radiusX, float
radiusY, int numSegments = 0 )
```

The preceding code draws a solid filled ellipse at the position defined in `position`. Radius along x axis is defined in `radiusX` and radius along y axis is defined in `radiusY`. `numSegments` is optional; that defines how many triangles are used for drawing the ellipse as this shape is drawn using OpenGL triangle fans. If it is `0`, the number of fans is decided automatically.

```
cinder::gl::drawStrokedEllipse( Vec2f position, float radiusX, float
radiusY, int numSegments = 0 )
```

The preceding code draws just the outline of an ellipse whose position is defined in `position`, radius along x axis in `radiusX`, radius along y axis in `radiusY`. and optionally, number of segments in `numSegments`.

```
cinder::gl::drawSolidRoundedRect( Rectf rect, float cornerRadius, int
numSegmentsPerCorner = 0 )
```

The preceding code draws a solid filled rectangle with rounded corners. Rectangle is defined in `rect`, its corner radius in `cornerRadius`, and it is possible to optionally define the number of segments that are used for drawing each corner in `numSegmentsPerCorner`. If it is set to `0`, the number of segments is decided automatically.

```
cinder::gl::drawStrokedRoundedRect( Rectf, float cornerRadius, int
numSegmentsPerCorner = 0 )
```

The preceding code draws just the outline of a rectangle with rounded corners. Rectangle is defined in `rect`, its corner radius in `cornerRadius`, and it is possible to optionally define the number of segments that are used for drawing each corner in `numSegmentsPerCorner`. If it is set to `0`, the number of segments is decided automatically.

To make these functions work, you have to import the OpenGL header file as follows:

```
#include "cinder/gl/gl.h"
```

Images

The following is the basic code that loads an image into a texture:

```
gl::Texture myTexture = gl::Texture( loadImage
   ( loadAsset( "image.png" ) ) );
```

This texture then is drawn within the `draw()` function by using the following code:

```
gl::draw( myTexture, Rectf(100,100,540,380) );
```

The first parameter is the texture that contains the loaded image, and the second parameter is rectangle that is drawn within the texture.

To make this code example work, you have to import the following header files:

```
#include "cinder/gl/gl.h"
#include "cinder/ImageIo.h"
#include "cinder/gl/Texture.h"
```

Other functions

Please refer to all the chapters in this book, if you are interested in 3D, video, sound, or other kinds of function reference as this kind of functionality makes use of classes, and the reference and explanation of these functions would take the same amount of space as the chapters.

If you want more of Cinder and you can't find what you are searching for in this book, please refer to the original Cinder function reference available at http://libcinder.org or one of many C++ or OpenGL language references. Another great place to look for help is the friendly *libcinder.org* forum.

As Cinder is open source, it is a good idea to look at the Cinder source code if you are in trouble and feel experienced enough to be able to find what you are searching for, or fix issues that are standing in your way.

This book is just a brief introduction of what is actually possible with Cinder.

Index

Symbols

3D drawing 89-92
3D primitives
 exploring 96-99
3D space 87, 88
#include statements 56, 68

A

ActionScript 8
addTrack() function 102
Apple Developer Account
 URL, for registration 10
ArcballDemo 26
Area object 57
assets
 handling 57-59
assets directory 58
audio
 visualizing 105-107
AudioGenerative 27
audio input
 using 108
audio::Output::play() method 102
audio::Source pointer 102
audio::SourceRef object 102
autoplay parameter 102

B

BaseApp 29
BaseApp class 122
BaseApp.sln file 39
BasicAnimation project
 circles, counting 68-70
 creating 61, 62
 multiple objects, animating 63-66
BasicApp 16, 17
basicApp.cpp file 16
BasicAudio project 101
BasicShapesApp.cpp 45
BasicShapes project
 about 45, 46
 circles, drawing 49-51
 lines, drawing 47-49
 rectangles, drawing 51
BezierPath 17-21
Boost libraries 8
built-in animation easing functions
 using 70-75

C

C++ 8
Cairo 21
CairoBasic
 about 21-23
 URL 21
CairoBasicApp.cpp file 22
CairoBasicShot.eps file 22
CairoBasicShot.pdf file 23
CairoBasicShot.ps file 23
CairoBasicShot.svg file 22
Cairo::createWindowSurface() function 42
CaptureTest 23
channel 77, 78

Channel class 78, 79
Channel.h file 79
Cinder
  about 8
  downloading 8, 9
  sample application, launching 13, 14
  setting, up on Mac OS X 10, 11
  setting, up on Windows 11
  setup, testing 13, 14
  URL 8
Cinder, functionality reference
  applications 122, 123
  basic graphics 124, 125
  basic images 126
  basic types 121
Cinder, setup on Windows
  DirectX SDK 12
  Microsoft Visual C++ Express 2010 11
  QuickTime SDK 12, 13
  Windows Platform SDK 11
Cinder, toolset
  ArcballDemo 26
  AudioGenerative 27
  BasicApp 16, 17
  BezierPath 17- 21
  CairoBasic 21-23
  CaptureTest 23
  Earthquake 26, 27
  EaseGallery 24
  TextBox 25
Cinder Version 0.8.4
  URL 9
Cinder Version 0.8.5
  URL 9
circles
  counting 68-70
  drawing 49-51
coding 7
Color object 46
console() function 119
CPU image processing
  versus GPU image processing 78
creative coder 7
creative coding 7

D

depth sorting
  handling 94, 95
dereferencing 116
DirectX SDK 12
dot-zero-f notation 17
drawColorCube() function 94
drawCube() function 91, 94
drawCylinder() function 98
drawing
  in 3D 89-92
drawing functions 52
draw() method 42, 46, 57, 62, 64, 79, 89, 92, 95, 111
drawSolidCircle() function 49, 50, 51, 62, 64, 98
drawSolidRect() function 51
drawSphere() function 97
drawStrokedCircle() function 50, 51
drawStrokedRect() function 51

E

Earthquake 26, 27
EaseGallery 24, 70
easeOutExpo() method 72
effect animation
  creating 82, 83
effects
  applying, to moving images 83-86
events
  handling 111, 112

F

fileDrop() event handler
  using 118, 119
fileDrop() method 112
Frustrum 88

G

getMousePos() method 113
getWindowBounds() method 57

getWindowCenter() method 49
getWindowHeight() function 47, 49
getWindowWidth() function 47, 49
gl::clear() function 46, 92
gl::clear() method 63, 89
gl::drawColorCube() function 96
gl::drawCube() function 90
gl::drawLine() function 47
glLineWidth() function 50
GPU 11
GPU image processing
  versus CPU image processing 78
grayscale effect
  applying 78-80

I

image
  loading 55-57
  loading, into texture 126

J

Java 8
JavaScript 8

K

keyDown() event handler
  using 118
keyDown() method 112
keyUp() method 112

L

lines
  drawing 47-49
loadAsset() function 58
loadUrl() function 58

M

Mac OS X
  Cinder, setting up on 10, 11
  project, creating from scratch 31

Mac OS X project
  code, adding 34
  connecting, to Cinder (Xcode 3) 35, 36
  connecting, to Cinder (Xcode 4+) 36-38
  Xcode 3 32, 33
  Xcode 4+ 33, 34
Microsoft Visual C++
  downloading 11
Microsoft Visual C++ Express 2010 11
modelview matrix 88
mouseDown() event handler
  using 114, 116
mouseDown() method 112, 115
mouseDrag() event handler
  using 116, 117
mouseDrag() method 112
mouseMove() event handler
  using 112, 113
mouseMove() method 103, 112
mouseUp() method 112
moving images
  effects, applying to 83-86
multiple objects
  animating, simultaneously 63-66

N

nested states 92-94

O

OpenGL 26, 88, 89
OpenGL Shading Language 78

P

PCM 105
PCM buffering
  enabling 106
popMatrices() function 91
popModelView() function 92
prepareSettings() method 62, 123
project
  setting up, in TinderBox 30, 31
projection 88

pulse code modulation. *See* PCM
pushMatrices() function 91
pushModelView() function 92 91

Q

QuadCore CPU 11
QuickTime Player
  URL, for downloading 13
QuickTime SDK 12, 13

R

random functions
  adding, in project 66, 68
rectangles
  drawing 51
RGB color system 46
rotate() function 90, 91

S

setup() method 41, 63, 80, 81, 95, 96, 111, 122
shaders 78
shutdown() method 122
sound file
  loading 101, 102
  playing 101, 102
SSD hard drive 11
surface 77, 78
Surface class 78

T

TextBox 25
texture
  about 77, 78
  image, loading into 126
Texture class 78
threshold
  using 80-82
TinderBox
  about 29, 45, 89
  BasicAnimation project, creating 61, 62
  project, setting up 30, 31
Track class 102

track parameters
  modifying 103-105
tracks
  using 102, 103
translate() function 91
TweenLite ActionScript library 24

U

update() method 41, 82, 95, 111, 122

V

Vec2f object 66
vector 114

W

Windows
  Cinder, setting up on 11
  project, creating from scratch 39, 40
Windows Platform SDK
  about 11
  downloading 11

X

Xcode 10
Xcode application 10

Thank you for buying
Cinder – Begin Creative Coding

About Packt Publishing

Packt, pronounced 'packed', published its first book "*Mastering phpMyAdmin for Effective MySQL Management*" in April 2004 and subsequently continued to specialize in publishing highly focused books on specific technologies and solutions.

Our books and publications share the experiences of your fellow IT professionals in adapting and customizing today's systems, applications, and frameworks. Our solution based books give you the knowledge and power to customize the software and technologies you're using to get the job done. Packt books are more specific and less general than the IT books you have seen in the past. Our unique business model allows us to bring you more focused information, giving you more of what you need to know, and less of what you don't.

Packt is a modern, yet unique publishing company, which focuses on producing quality, cutting-edge books for communities of developers, administrators, and newbies alike. For more information, please visit our website: www.packtpub.com.

About Packt Open Source

In 2010, Packt launched two new brands, Packt Open Source and Packt Enterprise, in order to continue its focus on specialization. This book is part of the Packt Open Source brand, home to books published on software built around Open Source licences, and offering information to anybody from advanced developers to budding web designers. The Open Source brand also runs Packt's Open Source Royalty Scheme, by which Packt gives a royalty to each Open Source project about whose software a book is sold.

Writing for Packt

We welcome all inquiries from people who are interested in authoring. Book proposals should be sent to author@packtpub.com. If your book idea is still at an early stage and you would like to discuss it first before writing a formal book proposal, contact us; one of our commissioning editors will get in touch with you.

We're not just looking for published authors; if you have strong technical skills but no writing experience, our experienced editors can help you develop a writing career, or simply get some additional reward for your expertise.

Cinder Creative Coding Cookbook

ISBN: 978-1-849518-70-3   Paperback: 300 pages

Create compelling graphics, animation, and interaction with Kinect and Camera input using one of the most powerful C++ frameworks available

1. Learn powerful techniques for building creative applications using motion sensing and tracking
2. Create applications using multimedia content including video, audio, images, and text
3. Draw and animate in 2D and 3D using fast performance techniques

Mastering openFrameworks: Creative Coding Demystified

ISBN: 978-1-849518-04-8   Paperback: 300 pages

Boost your creativity and develop highly-interactive projects for art, 3D, graphics, computer vision and more, with this comprehensive tutorial

1. A step-by-step practical tutorial that explains openFrameworks through easy to understand examples
2. Makes use of next generation technologies and techniques in your projects involving OpenCV, Microsoft Kinect, and so on
3. Sample codes and detailed insights into the projects, all using object oriented programming

Please check www.PacktPub.com for information on our titles

[PACKT] open source
community experience distilled
PUBLISHING

Dreamweaver CS5.5 Mobile and Web Development with HTML5, CSS3, and jQuery

ISBN: 978-1-849691-58-1   Paperback: 284 pages

Harness the cutting edge features of Dreamweaver for mobile and web development

1. Create web pages in Dreamweaver using the latest technology and approach
2. Add multimedia and interactivity to your websites
3. Optimize your websites for a wide range of platforms and build mobile apps with Dreamweaver

Processing 2: Creative Programming Cookbook

ISBN: 978-1-849517-94-2   Paperback: 306 pages

Over 90 highly-effective recipes to unleash your creativity with interactive art, graphics, computer vision, 3D, and more

1. Explore the Processing language with a broad range of practical recipes for computational art and graphics
2. Wide coverage of topics including interactive art, computer vision, visualization, drawing in 3D, and much more with Processing
3. Create interactive art installations and learn to export your artwork for print, screen, Internet, and mobile devices

Please check **www.PacktPub.com** for information on our titles

Made in the USA
Middletown, DE
22 September 2020